W9-CNQ-791

MAN POWER

THE NEW REVIVAL
IN AMERICA

MAN POWER

THE NEW REVIVAL IN AMERICA

▲

THE CALL TO AFRICAN AMERICAN MEN FOR SPIRITUAL REVIVAL

▼

Edwin Louis Cole

THOMAS NELSON PUBLISHERS
Nashville • Atlanta • London • Vancouver

Copyright © 1997 by Edwin Louis Cole

All rights reserved. Written permission must be secured from the publisher to use or reproduce any part of this book, except for brief quotations in critical reviews or articles.

Published in Nashville, Tennessee, by Thomas Nelson, Inc., Publishers, and distributed in Canada by Word Communications, Ltd., Richmond, British Columbia, and in the United Kingdom by Word (UK), Ltd., Milton Keynes, England.

Unless otherwise noted Scripture quotations are taken from THE NEW AMERICAN STANDARD BIBLE ®, © Copyright The Lockman Foundation 1960, 1962, 1963, 1968, 1971, 1972, 1973, 1975, 1977. Used by permission.

Scripture quotations noted NKJV are from the NEW KING JAMES VERSION of the Bible. Copyright © 1979, 1980, 1982, Thomas Nelson, Inc., Publishers.

Scripture quotations noted AMPLIFIED BIBLE are from THE AMPLIFIED BIBLE: Old Testament. Copyright © 1962, 1964 by Zondervan Publishing House (used by permission); and from THE AMPLIFIED NEW TESTAMENT. Copyright © 1958 by the Lockman Foundation (used by permission).

Scripture quotations noted NIV are taken from the HOLY BIBLE, NEW INTERNATIONAL VERSION ®. Copyright © 1973, 1978, 1984 by International Bible Society. Used by permission of Zondervan Bible Publishing House. All rights reserved.

The "NIV" and "New International Version" trademarks are registered in the United States Patent and Trademark Office by International Bible Society. Use of either trademark requires the permission of International Bible Society.

Scripture quotations noted CEV are from the CONTEMPORARY ENGLISH VERSION of the Bible © 1991, 1995 by the American Bible Society. Used by permission.

Portions of Ben Kinchlow's material were originally published in *You Don't Have to If You Don't Want To* © 1995 by Ben Kinchlow. Published by Thomas Nelson, Inc., Publishers. Used by permission.

Printed in the United States of America
1 2 3 4 5 6 7 QBK 03 02 01 00 99 98 97

DEDICATION

Dedicated to the new breed of men who are raising a standard for manhood and sparking a new
revival in America.

CONTENTS

ACKNOWLEDGMENTS

Special acknowledgment to the cross-cultural outreach of the International Christian Men's Network for inspiring the authors on the following pages, to Joann Webster for bringing this project together, to our friends at Thomas Nelson, to Honey Karr and Lois Bivins for checking references, and to Ken Walker for exercising his writing and editorial skills on behalf of many of the authors.

ACKNOWLEDGMENTS

Part One

THE RESURRECTION OF TRUE MANHOOD

Therefore if any man is in Christ, he is a new creature.

2 Corinthians 5:17

REAL MATURITY

by George Fitzgerald

I'm a man!"

The cry echoed throughout Brooklyn's Fort Greene and Bedford-Stuyvesant ghettos, where I became an adult. My older brother, Nelson, loved the boast because it masked the inadequacy he felt from being short. The rest of the neighborhood loved the words too. The surest way to provoke someone was to challenge his manhood. But, there was much more to manhood that we didn't learn on the streets. As I learned in the prison cell where the Bible and a book called *Maximized Manhood* changed my life, the measure of a man comes from things besides fighting, the ability to steal, and sexual prowess.

Manhood. The maturing of the young male. What does it mean? I will never forget when I read, *"Maturity doesn't come with age, but with the acceptance of responsibility."*[1] I struggled with that statement before I finally accepted its truth and the need to apply it to my life.

While I don't blame my actions on others, my upbringing did teach me irresponsibility. My natural father left when I was a baby. In kindergarten, I discovered my stepfather wasn't my real dad, but I had already developed a dislike for him because of his heavy drinking and abusive behavior.

Many pathetic role models filled our streets: drug dealers, pimps, gamblers, con artists, and hustlers. So did men who acted like my stepfather. He beat my mom, fathered more children than he could care for, and made money just to spend it on his selfish desires.

Surrounded by those role models, I adopted the same lifestyle. As a youngster, I stymied my emotional growth by refusing to accept any responsibility. I did no household chores, completed schoolwork only when I felt like it, and rebelled until I became insolent toward all authority. Even when there was a male figure in our home, I never saw any discipline, love, or self-respect.

Not until much later did I realize that my behavior came from basing my manhood on a value system that measures maturity by how much money you have in your pocket, how many babies you make, and how much you dominate the opposite sex.

Searching to Belong

After spending my early years in nearby Westchester County, we moved to Brooklyn when I was twelve. There I discovered I had earned a reputation by enduring a couple of years at an infamous juvenile home. I boosted the image by following one of the most feared gang leaders in Fort Greene. "Nazi" commanded respect. He never hesitated to cut or shoot anyone who challenged him—including the police.

He didn't lead me into crime, though. I made that decision myself. Because my family regularly moved to larger apartments as more money and space became available, I got tired of walking all over Brooklyn, especially on the turf of another gang. At thirteen, I stole my first car. Soon I added burglary to my list of skills.

These and other crimes led to a series of juvenile detention centers and training schools. Their attempts at behavior modification only turned into a revolving door. After six months of "rehabilitation," I'd spend six months on the streets with drug pushers, alcoholics, and gamblers, then get sent away for six more months.

Gangs thrived in the neighborhood and helped me learn to use my fists—a talent that paid off when I wound up at the Spotford Detention Facility in the Bronx. There I met Mr. Super, a huge-fisted supervisor who provoked me with streams of negative chatter. Once he taunted, "You'll never amount to anything."

"Oh yeah?" I challenged, squaring off to prove I could amount to something *right now*. Mr. Super licked me, but I got respect from the other detainees. They thought, *This guy is so tough and crazy that he'll fight the counselors*. Actually, I was scared to death of him, but I never showed it.

I got Mr. Super's respect too. He extended special privileges, like letting me pass out cigarettes and roam the halls when other guys were locked up. Though he knew I was conning him, he always gave me positive progress reports, because I kept dorm fights to a minimum. I knew what to say, how to act, and how to avoid problems that would extend my sentence.

As I neared my eighteenth birthday, I began hanging out with the "Five Percenters," an offshoot of the Black

Muslims. "Black Power" sounded cool, but what I really liked was their heavy use of marijuana.

Marijuana became a short step to heroin, which I started selling. A year later, the profits from heroin enabled me to start shooting it too. That touched off a twenty-year habit and continuing prison visits, with a cycle of forgery, robbery, credit card fraud, and drug charges.

Black Power

From a young age, I hated whites. Part of it was simply that all the district attorneys, judges, social workers, and others who sent me up were white. Another part was that my culture influenced me with stories of how "whitey" was responsible for the condition of blacks. Learning about the history of slavery drove me into deeper anger over blacks' seemingly hopeless conditions.

In my later teens, this hatred found an outlet in the guise of religion and cultural awareness offered by the Islamic faith. Soon, Black Muslim doctrine bounced around in my head, next to the militant, revolutionary, and hateful rhetoric of the Black Panthers. "Black Power," "Black Pride," and "self-determination" became the order of the day.

After a while, I shifted to the so-called orthodox branch of Islam, the Sunni Muslims. Though I attempted to discipline myself with religious rituals like quoting the Al-Fatiah, learning to speak and read Arabic, and praying to Mecca five times a day, I discovered no real inner peace or maturity.

Two factors led me to break with the Muslims. Because the Big Apple's jails were overflowing, for one nine-month term the city sent me to Dannemora, a prison for hardened criminals in upstate New York. There I saw one of the men accused of shooting Malcolm X. Rumors flew about who was responsible for the crime. Though I never talked to the alleged gunman, I still considered Malcolm a hero. So I didn't care for the Muslim hit man or his religion.

The second factor came from a dispute over the Qur'an's account of Jesus' virgin birth, which I loved to read and research.[2] When I questioned why it didn't line up with a commentary on the Qur'an, the Imam, their pastor, told me I should put more faith in the commentary than in the holy book.

I didn't like that and told him so. In a religious atmosphere that teaches followers to blindly follow their leaders, my Islamic superiors branded me "insubordinate" and ostracized me from the community.

So much for religion. I no longer wanted anything to do with any sect. No longer tolerant of religious jargon or "cultural awareness," and fed up with the constant struggle for survival, I developed an insensitivity toward everything I considered spiritual.

Hitting Bottom

Looking back, I see that a "do your own thing" attitude is an illusion. Men will either do God's thing or Satan's thing. For years, I chose Satan's thing but believed I was my own master. The consequences included a drug habit that robbed me of dignity and freedom, plus thirteen years in prison, which I served off and on during the twenty-three years between 1967 and 1990. I call it doing life on the installment plan.

Maturity eluded me. My search for complete independence from society's dictates led to failure in all my relationships, including those with my immediate family, friends, wife, and, for many years, my children.

I fathered my first son at age twenty with Ruth, the woman who is now my wife. When I married another woman at twenty-seven, it was primarily in the hope of looking better in court when I stood trial on armed robbery charges. I was only the getaway driver, but since I refused to snitch on my brother and his friend, the state rewarded me with a five-to ten-year sentence.

I was constantly paroled for one crime, then back in for another, and I was high as much of the time as possible. It was a miserable, unfulfilling way of life, yet one that I was powerless to change in my self-driven, drug-induced fog.

The change began on New Year's Eve as 1986 drew to a close. By then my marriage had crumbled, and I had moved to Dallas, to live again with Ruth. Despite having changed communities, I continued to hustle for a living. My antics drove Ruth to the verge of suicide.

In desperation one night, she called out to God. God says in his Word, "Call to Me, and I will answer you, and I will tell you great and mighty things, which you do not know."[3] Before I knew what happened, Ruth proclaimed she had accepted Jesus and joined a church. She came to me, her eyes glinting fire, with this ultimatum: "Get saved or get gone!"

I ran! Upset that I couldn't be with my woman, I drove to North Carolina to spend time with my three daughters. But they didn't want anything to do with me, either. Distraught, I hit the highway for months. Stealing and forging checks along the way to get drugs, I soon returned to mainlining heroin. I wound up in Savannah, Georgia, a complete mess.

Holed up in a hotel room and strung out on a ten-day high, I felt so depressed and desperate that I cried out to the Lord the same way Ruth had. Stretching out my arms, I pleaded, "God, either save me or destroy me!" After throwing my drug paraphernalia in the trash, I fell across the bed, longing for sleep that I hadn't been able to get.

I awoke the next morning and reasoned that since God hadn't destroyed me, he must have saved me. I had heard just enough throughout my life to know that Jesus was the Son of God and the way to salvation. I affirmed my acceptance of him with a single prayer, and he immediately spoke to my heart about what I should do next: confess my crimes and suffer the consequences.

Though I was guilty of a variety of crimes, the outstanding federal warrant against me was for cashing stolen social security checks. I phoned the police to let them know I was turning myself in. Then I called Ruth to let her know I was as saved as I knew how to be.

When she heard the news that I had called on God, she shrieked for joy. She became the first member of a strong support network that enabled me to begin growing during what would be my last prison term. Because we believed God would release me before my sentence was up, Ruth and I got married while I was still imprisoned so that afterward, we could reunite as husband and wife.

A New Man

In prison, God revealed himself to me in powerful ways that, in the past, I wouldn't have believed possible. He began making me "a new creature" in Christ.[4] Simultaneously, he gave me hope by letting me know he had a plan for my life.[5] This plan included real maturity in my attitudes, behavior, speech, and character—a radical transformation from the man I was into the man he wanted me to be.

Drastic changes occurred as I devoured the words of Jesus. All I wanted to read was what he said, which in my Bible was printed in red. I eventually saw that manhood comes when we pattern ourselves after Jesus, not the world's role models. I began discussing the truths of God's Word with whomever would listen. Many suspected it to be just another con, yet they couldn't deny the reality of this once rage-filled drug addict transforming into a responsible, mature, loving, peaceful man.

> *Manhood has nothing to do with my age or color but everything to do with becoming accountable for my actions.*

Four months after I went to prison, Ruth sent me *Maximized Manhood*. I read that book several times and realized I wasn't even *minimized* in my manhood because of my rebellion and lack of responsibility. I hadn't been responsible to anyone in authority. I believed that all black men were threatened by those in authority because our independence had been denied for so long.

Through that book, I saw the need to accept responsibility for my actions and become as much like Christ as I possibly could. I realized manhood had nothing to do with age or color and everything to do with becoming accountable for my actions—not only to the Lord, but also to my brothers and sisters in the family of God.

Continuing to study the Bible, I took to heart these words of Jesus: "If anyone wishes to come after Me, let him deny himself, and take up his cross, and follow Me."[6] How humbling it was to deny myself and acknowledge my dependence on him to show me the way!

It wasn't easy. He directed me to ask for forgiveness from my family and friends, confessing my failure for not being the husband, father, son, or man I should have been. Though most treated my apologies favorably, one of my sons watched me skeptically for two years after my release before I convinced him of my sincerity.

While the Lord was humbling me and revealing himself to me inside prison, he was restoring and developing my relationships on the outside as well. He put me directly in touch with the author of *Maximized Manhood*, Edwin Louis Cole, who gave me my first job after I was paroled. Volunteers with Prison Fellowship came to help strengthen me, and men of God like A. R. Bernard encouraged me and shared their scriptural insights.

I saw the Lord's power in the way he placed those people in my life and orchestrated everything once I surrendered to him. The most outstanding example was my supernatural prison release.

Confined in Georgia, I had applied for a transfer to Texas so I could be closer to Ruth. I kept after the authorities, seeking transfer hearings six times and enlisting pastors, friends, and other supporters to write letters on my behalf. The parole board got so fed up that the prison officials warned me, "We don't want another letter on this case or you'll do a minimum of fifteen years."

I remained convinced that God would free me, so I chose to trust him and stopped appealing to a human system. A month later, I received a letter from the board that had previously denied me a transfer six times. "We are paroling you from your sentence," it said. It gave no explanation, and I didn't request one. I knew the Lord had divinely intervened on my behalf.

After serving less than three years of a twenty-year sentence—a sentence that was supposed to carry a minimum of twelve years and was given by officials who promised they would not parole me—I was set free!

I compare that miracle to the time when God sent an angel to release the apostle Peter from prison.[7] For me, the Lord sent an angel in the form of a corrections lieutenant. She came and opened my cell door at 3 A.M., processed me out of prison, and gave me a one-way ticket to Dallas.

My predawn entrance to freedom still amazes me. The procedure she followed was unheard of in the federal corrections system. I saw the Lord's hand all over it. Besides filling me with joy, it confirmed my witness to other inmates with whom I had discussed the Bible, including those who had ridiculed me.

Since then, I've seen many inmates with whom the Lord has dealt very differently. Some He uses inside prison walls, and some He keeps there because He knows they couldn't handle the temptations on the outside. Others he releases, and some he even pardons before they spend a day behind bars. He deals with each of us right where we are.

The Real You

God has performed a wealth of miracles in my life since my release from prison. How else can you explain a convict of long standing becoming a minister of the gospel? I first learned about ministering to men as part of the Christian Men's Network. After that, I became the associate pastor of The Jesus Center in Arlington, Texas.

After four years of training and maturing in my Christian walk, the Lord showed me it was time to move into evangelism. Following His direction, I started

What matters is not who you think you are, being "the man." What matters is who you really are.

Wake Up Ministry, which concentrates on sharing the good news of Christ with young people and men. My oldest son, Everett, travels with me, performing Christian rap tunes before I testify and preach the gospel.

Who am I to do something like that? Just a man who loves God. Today I can confidently say that what matters is not who you think you are, being "the man." What matters is who you really are.

Despite all the religious rhetoric that fills the air these days, God's Word is clear and sure. His love will wash away hatred, bitterness, and resentment. Ironically, God used white men to help disciple me. Racial prejudice is a historical fact, but it's not a piece of baggage we have to carry.

I don't need human doctrine to convince me that God loves us all, regardless of race or color. He tells me that Himself. In His Word, the apostle John wrote, "After these things I looked, and behold, a great multitude, which no one could count, from every nation and all tribes and peoples and tongues, standing before the throne and before the Lamb, clothed in white robes."[8]

Those standing before God's throne are from all nations and peoples. Grasp the truth of this Scripture and you'll be able to give up human power struggles for the overcoming power of God. Then you can stand proud, regardless of your background, and be sure of your manhood.

Since leaving prison, I've been brought into the company of some truly great men. Bishop Eddie Long is one of God's champions, and he has more light to shed on the idea of real manhood.

2

THE NEW REVIVAL IN AMERICA

by Eddie Long

I learned the hard way what God really wanted out of a man. I'll never forget my oldest son's third birthday. Like all toddlers, he was excited, but I had little to celebrate. I was mired in a marriage I couldn't stand, yet because I was a pastor, I could not simply divorce. Attempts at reconciling our differences only touched off more arguments. The strain left me in such turmoil that I finally shook my head and prayed, "Lord, I can't leave, but I can't take it any longer."

I made crazy, desperate plans to check out. I daydreamed of coming home one afternoon, shooting my wife, killing my son, and turning the gun on myself. Such thoughts flitted through my mind as I brought my boy home from his party. As I turned the key and pushed open the front door, a shock ripped through me. The house looked as if burglars had stripped it clean. But the only "intruder" that day had been my wife. She had cleaned out and taken off.

When I finally found her, we took a more civil way out of the situation than murder—divorce court. But I might as well have died for all the eulogies church members said over me: "Well, preacher, we're real sorry about that." "You'll never pastor again." "God can't use you now. You're divorced." "What are you going to do for a job?"

That was a decade, two churches, and thousands of members ago. After folks in the congregation tuned me out, I listened to God. He said to my heart: *Get it together, Long, and come on with me. Come and you will find rest. My yoke is easy, and my burden is light.*

I was ready to obey. Failure humbles you. And I felt like an utter failure. So I had to quit relying on old methods and traditions and start looking for real answers. I found them in a real God.

I grew so dependent on God that I actually relied on him for sermons instead of my intellect and ability. "Lord," I often sighed as the week wore on and no Scriptures had inspired me, "I've been reading a lot and studying, but nothing's hooked me yet. I just can't preach a sermon. If I haven't touched it, felt it, and lived it, I can't talk it. But Lord, I believe you won't let me or the folks here down. You put me here. This is your church, and I'm just your assistant."

He never failed me. Now, whenever I struggle for a message, face tough decisions, or am about to enter a meeting where tempers are sure to boil, I look to him. I tell the Lord that he set it up, and I expect him to give me my role. Just as He promised, his burden is light. When I don't have to make all the decisions but just open myself to Him to finish the work, it's amazing how smoothly life flows. He never failed me, and he won't fail you, either.

The same thing that God said to me during those dark days He says to all men today. To summarize his word very simply, God says, *I'm not looking for perfection, I'm looking for hearts. I know you don't have everything right. But turn your heart toward me, come with me, and I'll fix everything else.*

That's what our society craves—for God to fix our problems. Look around at the plagues of murder, rape, drugs, violence, poverty, homelessness, hunger, and countless other ills. It doesn't take a genius to see that we have major problems.

A Lazarus Life

Lazarus is the man Christ raised from the dead after three days in a tomb (see John 11). Considering what God has done in my life, I call myself a Lazarus. I came to life when most people considered me dead.

Between my arrival at New Birth Missionary Baptist Church in 1987 and the present, the Lord increased our congregation from 300 members to almost 14,000, with a budget totaling $7.5 million. I'm not bragging. I never had a master plan, and that includes not having a plan to manage our latest budget. When we held a leadership meeting in October 1994 to look at the coming year, we had no agenda. We met for two days of prayer and listened to the CEO upstairs. When we adjourned, we knew what to do.

Besides the Bible, the only book I used for guidance in the early days at this church was *Maximized Manhood*. I sponsored men's meetings when only a handful of men showed up. Yet I forged ahead, determined to drive home the message that great churches—like great cities, states, and nations—are built on strong men. Today, instead of the customary church ratio of two females for every man, our population is 43 percent male.

Those aren't just male bodies occupying a pew, either, but active, dynamic men. They volunteer to mentor young males, primarily those in high school but some as young as elementary age. They eat lunch with them at least twice a month, follow their progress, and help them to find jobs.

You don't have to be young to be helped at New Birth, though. If someone is unemployed, our men are committed to helping him (or her) find a job. This extends to the individuals in our prison ministry, which offers scriptural teaching, job training, and counseling for drug-related problems (since drugs account for 80 percent of crime). When the inmates we help are released from jail, they have a job and a home waiting for them.

This is why I say that when a man gets excited about God, he becomes the greatest social tool a community could ever hope to see and the greatest evangelistic tool a church could ever want.

But what happened in our congregation didn't come from inspirational writings, church-growth seminars, or our natural brilliance. Our success began with God's plan for us as described in Genesis: "Then God said, 'Let Us make man in Our image, according to Our likeness; and let them rule over the fish of the sea and over the birds of the sky and over the cattle and over all the earth, and over every creeping thing that creeps on the earth.' And God created man in His own image."[1]

When God got ready to build his first nation, he started with a man. He needed a foundation. Compare it to a multimillion-dollar conference center. Before workers install the platforms, raise the walls, erect the partitions, hang the ceiling, and wire the lights, they must lay a foundation. It has to be strong enough to support everything that will be lifted onto it.

So it is with men. In Genesis, God started with man as a foundation. That means we are strong enough to support everything he builds on us. Because of him, we can handle the stress of job responsibilities, children, homes, wives, political conflicts, church squabbles, injustices, prejudices, and whatever else the world may throw at us.

From man came woman, and from woman came child. God created man from the earth, but when he created woman, he took her out of man. When he created children, he took them out of the woman. Everything started from the foundation of the man.

The biggest problem in today's society, and in the body of Christ, is men who refuse to fulfill the foundational responsibility that God created for them. Instead of strong men, we have a lot of plastic men—ones who melt when things get too hot. God says to men as individuals, as a church, and as a society, "Every pain and stress I put on you, you will be able to handle."[2]

Rather than facing the stress, though, too many men simply get stressed out. They run to drugs, sleep, sex, sports, food, money, exotic vacations, and gambling, all the while moaning, "The pressure is too much!" In the heavens, God shakes his head and says, "No. I made you first. You're the foundation. You can handle everything that comes your way."

Because there are so many shrill voices attacking men and trying to rob them of their masculinity, many men fail to understand that they really can hold up—not because of their own strength, but through God. Perseverance is a gift from him.

And all is not lost. God is unleashing a massive tidal wave of help for men—from the Christian Men's Network to Promise Keepers to Bishop T.D. Jakes' Men's conferences. As this revival sweeps across the country, it cries to men like the voice of Jesus, saying, "Lazarus, come forth!"

The Buck Stops Here

Problems like murder, drugs, broken homes, degradation, and churches that are so lost they fail even to preach the basics of the gospel have inflicted pain and suffering on our society. These troubles aren't unique to my hometown of Atlanta. They exist in New York, Chicago, Miami, Seattle, Los Angeles, and thousands of cities and towns in between.

Even though the problems are national in scope, however, we can't understand or resolve them nationally. They begin with us—with men. If we go back to the state level and look around the state, any state, we see murder, rape, drugs, and crime. If we look a little closer at the city, any city, we see murder, rape, drugs, and crime, including a host of black-on-black crime. Trace it to the city's basic unit—the neighborhoods. There, too, we see these crimes and their effects. Then look at those in real trouble today—the children. Who guides them? Look at the women and you see the pain and suffering. That leaves only one place to search. The man.

President Harry Truman had a sign on his desk that read, "The buck stops here." Brother, the buck stops with us! The root of our problems lies at the heart of the foundation.

To address society's problems, I had to help straighten out the foundation, and to do that I had to concentrate on men. My new wife used to complain, "You don't give the women enough attention." I replied, "Honey, if I fix the men, won't that solve at least 80 percent of the women's problems?" Strong men make for strong families, which is America's crying need.

To be effective with men, I had to learn to understand them and how God created them. Men basically aren't emotional. Sure, we may cry at funerals or get choked up at our daughter's wedding, but we are essentially rational thinkers. If you're a pastor, and you don't have many men in your church, check how you're preaching. If you're more interested in how many in the congregation shout and sway than in how many stay around to think, you can forget about men.

A man will go where he faces a challenge for his intellect and spirit. That realization made me change. When I got into the pulpit, I had to tell the men, "Thus saith the Lord." I had to confront the men with God's Word.

Not only did I have to address them directly from Scripture, but I also had to ensure that the images in front of them didn't distract them. For years in the African-American community, the preacher carried the image of a pimp. Think about it. A man went into church for the first time and saw three ladies dressed in white chasing this preacher around, putting handkerchiefs on his brow, and serving his every need. *Bad image.*

That's why men meet me at the door on Sunday morning. Men carry my books. Men bring me a glass of water. What these men and I are doing is rebuilding a strong masculine image for Christianity in our community, which is essential if we're ever to have strong families again.

Black History

To see how the African-American culture is related to strong families, we need to look at our history—not our African history, but our American history.

Estimates of those slaves who reached America alive between the sixteenth and nineteenth centuries range from 8 to 15 million; that means more than 80 percent of those on slave ships died.

We must rebuild a strong masculine image for Christianity in our community if we're ever going to have strong families again.

Now, you can focus on this tragedy, or you can think about those who survived. If brutality, starvation, and chains didn't kill them, what were they? *Strong.* That means your great-great-great-grandpa and your great-great-great-grandma came from sturdy stock.

Even the end of slavery didn't halt poor living conditions. Study the history of sharecropping. Our strong ancestors knew it was a bad deal, but they said, "It may put us at a disadvantage economically, but at least we can hold our families together." They put family ahead of self-interest and righteousness ahead of economics. Today, on the other hand, we see impressive economic advances for millions of African-Americans, but at what cost? Our families are falling apart!

What motivated our ancestors? Not just human love, because that kind of self-driven source quickly runs out of gas. There was a spiritual element that can't be overlooked. Again, this lesson comes from our history.

Slavery was so oppressive that in most areas of the South, it was illegal to teach slaves how to read and write. Small wonder that in 1880, some 70 percent of blacks were still illiterate; only 30 percent could read. Yet between 1880 and 1910, those figures were completely reversed.

In just thirty years, 70 percent of blacks could read. Why? Because former slaves, along with their children and grandchildren, learned to read for the sole purpose of reading one book—the Bible. Without a government program, school vouchers, or a national literacy campaign, a revolution took place. In the midst of a lack of employment, few voting rights, and the rise of the Ku Klux Klan, a whole culture turned from being illiterate to literate. All because of the Bible.

Yet look at what's happening now. We learned to read and forgot the book that told us how to act. Consequently, in America's major metropolitan areas today, the overwhelming majority of African-Americans' problems come from the failure to keep our families together. Despite overwhelming odds, we kept our families intact for centuries. Until 1960, most homes were headed by two parents. But today's norm is "single mother, head of household."

What a shame that is to us! Having been through so much and endured, we now have lost our families, our communities, our jobs, and our position. Worse, we have lost a people whom God had made strong—not superior, but strong enough to survive what he knew we would face.

God called us to be a standard, but instead we're letting our enemy the devil lock up many of us—if not in prison, then in the muck and mire of drugs and despair that make us just as worthless. Some complain, "Well, the reason for this stuff is that there are no jobs. Racism is holding us down and keeping us back." But I would ask, when *haven't* we faced racism? When *wasn't* there a lack of jobs and economic opportunity?

When we got to where God wanted us—when we could use the same bathrooms, eat at the same lunch counters, ride in any seat on the bus, and work in all kinds of jobs—we forgot Him. When we lost sight of God, we lost sight of our heritage and our future.

If anyone should know there is a God, it's black people. Only the Lord would give the ingenuity to start with a chicken foot, fry it up one day, stew it the next day, and make dumplings the third day. Yet, when we got to where God wanted us—when we could use the same bathrooms, eat at the same lunch counters, ride in any seat on the bus, and work in all kinds of jobs—we forgot him.

When we lost sight of God, we lost sight of our heritage and our future. We made it intact to 1960 not because we were smart, held lots of "Fortune 500" jobs, or had a savior in the White House. We came through because we put our trust in the God who created us. We leaned solely on him.

In years past, we were a people driven by morals and the Spirit of God. Now we're driven by economics, and our morals are shot. We even get up in our pulpits and constantly preach prosperity, crossing the line between God's Word and greed. We can't measure our spirituality by "how much" or "how many." Your grandparents didn't measure their lives by the size of their paychecks or their suburban homes. First they chose to do what was right.

Lack of Self

Fortunately, revival is spreading across America. It's happening because many are dying to themselves. They don't run around screaming, "I want!" Instead they are asking, "What does God want?" They have died to the all-out pursuit of pleasure and materialism. They are telling their children, "Do this because it's the right thing to do," not "Do this because you can make some money."

Why have so many of our children sold drugs in recent years? Drugs aren't new. Guns aren't new. Still, in the past most kids didn't touch them because they knew it wasn't right. They didn't want to hurt someone else. Now, even though drugs are destroying millions of lives, they don't see that. Their eyes are on the money. They see economic gain, which is merely a tool for what they really want—personal pleasure. The pursuit of pleasure is the root of our society's pain, and it's killing our nation.

> ▲ ▲ ▲ ▲ ▲
>
> *God is calling men who will put Him first, who are tired of worldly games, who are willing to do the right thing simply because it's the right thing.*
>
> ▼ ▼ ▼ ▼ ▼

However, we can't let despair overwhelm us. After all, you can't resurrect something unless it's dead. If we didn't have problems, we wouldn't need revival. I'm not excited about the problems we still face, but I *am* excited that God is acting to overcome them!

He is calling men who will put him first, who are tired of worldly games, who are willing to do the right thing simply because it's the right thing.

The words God spoke to me after my divorce were right out of Scripture: "My yoke is easy, and My load is light."[3] He also says, "Come to Me, all who are weary and heavy-laden, and I will give you rest. Take My yoke upon you, and learn from Me, for I am gentle and humble in heart; and you shall find rest for your souls."[4]

That's the promise of revival. Not everybody wants it. Not everyone will join in or greet it gladly. But God is saying, "Those of you who are fed up with going through the motions, I have a revival going on in which I'm giving life. You who are tired of not seeing anything, who know there's more, who want to turn and offer yourselves to me—those of you who want to be real with me, come on!"

In the next chapter, LaFayette Scales will give you the overall picture of what it means to be a strong, revived man. I urge you to read on, get real with God, and fulfill your manhood starting *today*.

3

REDISCOVERING MANHOOD

by LaFayette Scales

We live in a dangerous era, one that can be compared to the days of Ezekiel. That ancient prophet told of a land whose priests, princes, advisers, and people violated the law, dabbled in occult practices, profaned God's name, and oppressed others. Sounds like today.

Ezekiel also gave God's solution: to seek for a man among them to stand in the gap and hold back God's judgment. Yet, he couldn't find one.[1]

The world teaches that men have evolved. But the parallels between today and the world of six thousand years ago show that we haven't progressed one bit. God created men to rule. Instead, we're still tossed to and fro like leaves in an autumn breeze. We often see the following types of males:

Marshmallow Men: Men who don't know their potential.
Macho Men: Men who misuse their abilities.
Mixed Men: Men who don't know their identity.

But the world cries out for:

Mighty Men: Men who are strong in the Lord and know the power of His might.

As we near the end of the twentieth century, America lurches and stumbles like a lost waif, caught in the throes of a manhood crisis. We have too many males who have grown in years, but still, as the Bible says, speak like children, understand like children, and think like children.[2] We desperately need men with solutions, men who will ask five penetrating questions:

Identity:	Who am I?
Source:	Where did I come from?
Purpose:	Why am I here?
Potential:	What can I do?
Hope:	Where am I going?

Men with the answers to these questions can lead this generation out of its dilemmas.

My father died when I was eight years old, leaving my mother to raise three children. My father was an usher, a deacon, and a servant in the church. Upon the death of my father, the men of the church rallied around me to teach me, by example and by association, the various areas of manhood.

George Burden would adopt me as a son and take me to the annual father and son banquet to give me *identity* with men. Calvin Ward was the Sunday school teacher who taught me that my *source* was God and I must trust Him. Harold Shank was my scoutmaster and taught me to stretch beyond my own limitations and press into my *potential*.

Phale D. Hale, our pastor, helped me to set my *hope* in God, for the present and future, by preaching and living an exemplary life. John Sanders, our assistant pastor, helped me to discover my *purpose* in ministry, carefully laying down the foundation for a Christ-centered ministry.

Through these men I was able to answer life's five big questions. The Lord sent them into my life. God says in his word, "When my father and my mother forsake me, then the LORD will take me up."[3]

Because of these and many other men in my life, I was able to avoid many of the traps young men from single-parent homes encounter. God's men of today still have a responsibility to take up the young men and help them answer the five big questions. All men, young and old, must discover and walk in their manhood.

The Five Big Questions

Identity. America collectively scratches its head, grappling with the plague of riotous behavior on its streets, wondering why there are so many danger zones and lawless jungles where even the police fear to tread. Some say we have a drug problem; others, a money problem. Some believe our crisis stems from economics. Still others blame it on politics. I call it a *father* problem. Why? Because fathers give us our identity. With too few fathers to pass on identity to their children, kids are left to run wild.

This also has spiritual consequences. The greatest tragedy of today is that millions can't grasp the loving nature of their heavenly Father because their image of "father" has been spoiled by the abuse or neglect of their earthly dad. Those who suffer from that must turn to God and ask him to help them forgive their fathers and find the acceptance they seek in his love.

The identity question must be resolved. *Men can't lead until they understand that their true identity comes from their heavenly Father.*

We need to identify ourselves with God.

Source. The prophet Jeremiah described an earth in crisis: without form, in chaos, void, empty of purpose, and lacking light. The mountains and hills trembled and moved.[4] Why? *There was no man!* He spoke of a time when cities were broken down and desolate. A once fruitful land had dried up into a desert. The earth mourned, the heavens turned dark, everyone fled from the cities, and cries and groans of anguish filled the air.[5] God's solution was to go through the streets of Jerusalem to find a man who would seek truth and execute judgment.[6]

In every generation the Lord's solution comes from his foreknowledge of the future. He looks down the road of history and sees the crises, confusion, and challenges yet to come. Then he causes a man to be born who, in time, will seek him, find Him, and receive him. Such a man receives the answer to his source question: *he discovers he came from God.*[7]

We need to know we were created as unique beings by God. No one else can be you.

Purpose. God created man to have dominion over the earth. He began with Adam in the testing place, the Garden of Eden. If Adam proved his worthiness there, the world awaited him. But he didn't fulfill God's mandate to replenish the earth, subdue it, and bring everything in it under his authority. God is still looking for men to carry out the mandate.

To have dominion means to exert mastery, control, reign, or rule over. Fear, threats, disease, and anxiety don't stand up to this authority. Man cannot fulfill his purpose through a jigger, a jug, or a joint. God made us superior to tobacco, grapes, hops, barley, marijuana, and coca plants. Men rank above copper, nickel, silver, gold, wood, and any other resources used to coin money.

When man meets God, he discovers he was made to serve God.

We need to find our specific purpose in exercising authority over the earth. No one else can do what you alone were designed to do.

Potential. The man who meets God also finds the answer to his question "What can I do?" The answer is, everything! All things are possible with God.[8] And why not? God created man in his own image.[9] God encompasses creativity, productivity, and industry. He is love, truth, and goodness—full of mercy and righteousness. King David said, "I am fearfully and wonderfully made."[10] *God's grace equips a man with the ability to be a solution for his generation.*

Man's potential can be defined as unrealized possibilities—what he is capable of, but has not yet shown. Our potential is in our hidden ability, our untapped resources, and our unused success. Today's generation demands only to see our visible ability. But we can respond *beyond* that by meeting the God who calls us, by faith, to maximize our potential.

The Lord designs every man to do what no one else has done in his generation. He is "able to do exceeding abundantly beyond all that we ask or think, according to the power that works within us."[11]

When we understand the power within that comes from God's grace, we're able to take responsibility for that power. Men with this awareness are accountable to God, as well as to their generation. They take responsibility, which I call *the right response to the ability within me.*

You need to accept responsibility to fulfill your potential. If you don't do it, no one else will.

Hope. Men who meet God have a settled past, a sure present, and a favorable future. Since they know where they're going, they forget where they've been and cling to hope—trust and expectation for favorable change. They're like Paul, who wrote, "But one thing I do: forgetting what lies behind and reaching forward to what lies ahead, I press on toward the goal for the prize of the upward call of God in Christ Jesus."[12]

With hope, man will plan. Reaching and stretching today, he has expectant confidence in tomorrow. Instead of wasting time, he uses it. Based on hope, time can be a great tool. In Ecclesiastes, King Solomon tells us there is a time to be born and a time to die. *But a man with hope believes God has given him enough time to finish his course.*

Paul wrote, "I have fought the good fight, I have finished the course, I have kept the faith; in the future there is laid up for me the crown of righteousness, which the Lord, the righteous Judge, will award to me on that day; and not only to me, but also to all who have loved His appearing."[13] The hope expressed in this passage reflects the knowledge of destiny, which provides an anchor for our soul in times of trouble. Hope keeps us from dropping out and giving up.

You need to see beyond your earthly circumstances into the destiny God has for you. No one else can fill it but you.

God knew a crisis would come to earth in the 1990s, so he birthed men in the '20s, '30s, '40s, '50s, '60s, '70s, and '80s who would meet him in time and settle the questions of identity, source, purpose, potential, and hope. These men will bring the solutions to the world's crises.

In their generations, God created a program and designated men with the answers. They are here—somewhere. But why aren't they in the house of the Lord? Why aren't they fulfilling their destiny? One reason is that too many men have been deceived into thinking their source is a nation—be that in Africa, Asia, or Europe—and are caught in a cultural trap. Instead of exercising dominion, others lie in bondage to drugs, alcohol, and sex. Still others, because they've never answered life's critical questions, are misusing their potential and abilities.

God said he would have spared Sodom and Gomorrah for the sake of ten righteous men, but he couldn't find them. The Bible says, "For the eyes of the LORD move to and fro throughout the earth that He may strongly support those whose heart is completely His."[14] Today, God is looking in the streets for men he birthed for this reason, to provide solutions to our urban blight, to model manhood to a generation, and to change the world. Men have a responsibility to their generation. We must become the mature men the world needs.

The New, Mature Fathers

When the members of the church at Corinth squabbled among themselves over whom they followed—some Paul, others Cephas or Apollos—the apostle Paul wrote them a letter of correction. "Did any of those people die for you on the cross?" he asked. None of them were anything except ministers of the Lord Jesus Christ. He reminded them, "After all, though you should have ten thousand [leaders] in Christ, yet you do not have many fathers."[15]

Today God is looking for men to provide solutions to our urban blight, to model manhood to a generation, and to change the world. Men have a responsibility to their generation. We must become the mature men the world needs.

Fathers are the men who train you, not just sire you.
God told man to be fruitful and multiply and also to take dominion over the earth. Many men want to embrace the fruitful part and forget the training! I know men running around my city of Columbus, Ohio, who have tried personally to fulfill God's mandate to be fruitful! But any farmer can tell you the truth: *You don't just plant a crop and forget about it.* You nurture it, water it, prune it, and trust God to bring the growth.

The word *father* comes from the Hebrew word *ab*, which we call "abba," meaning "father" or "daddy." The rich, full meaning of this word is "progenitor," or someone who has genes, or life, inside himself. At its root, *father* means "source."

Our world desperately needs fathers, men who have life and know where they came from. We have a lot of folks who express their heartfelt desire to return to the African motherland. But I don't want to go back to my mother! The motherland doesn't give me identity. Identity comes from the seed, which resides in the father.

Mothers give children necessary nurturing with gentleness and affection. But from a father comes a child's sense of destiny, backbone, and strength of character to stand alone. Fathers tell us who we are. Millions of children across America are crying out for their fathers, or at least for men who will care for them.

But change is coming. Malachi said that in the last days, God would turn the hearts of the fathers to the children, and the hearts of the children to the fathers.[16] I see this happening all around me today.

The deliverance of wisdom and anointing from father to son, leader to follower, and prophet to pupil rests on biblical example. Elijah passed on his anointing to Elisha, whom he loved and instructed as if he were his natural son.[17] This parallels the examples of Moses and Joshua, Aaron and his sons, Paul and Timothy, and Christ and his followers. *Every father, whether biological or spiritual, has methods, messages, and a ministry of manhood that need to flow to a son.*

▲ ▲ ▲ ▲ ▲

Every father, whether biological or spiritual, has methods, messages, and a ministry of manhood that need to flow to a son.

▼ ▼ ▼ ▼ ▼

In our church, we bring old and young men together through a ministry known as Young Men of Destiny. We couple the wisdom of mature men with the strength of young men. God has blessed this effort. We have seen many biological and spiritual father-son relationships grow. Older men are discipling the younger ones in spirit, soul, and body, and in family, social, and financial issues. Gathering one on one, in small groups, and in larger meetings, men are receiving valuable instruction and inspiration.

The African-American Wise Man

"When I was a child, I used to speak as a child, think as a child, reason as a child; when I became a man, I did away with childish things."[18] Look at the childish things we must put away.

Children start out life not knowing how to talk or walk and are simpleminded. You are born a male child, but you must grow into a man. As Ben Kinchlow says, "Being a male is a matter of birth; being a man is a matter of choice."[19]

The first several chapters of Proverbs describe man in three stages: (1) a simple man, (2) a wise man, and (3) a fool. Simple men lack knowledge and experience. When a man answers and follows the call to wisdom, he advances from a simpleminded state to wisdom. But when a simple man rejects or ignores this call, he becomes a fool, a person empty of knowledge. Our streets are full of fools and simpletons. Yet those men have the potential to become wise and change our cities if they will hear, pursue, and embrace wisdom.

Childish Speaking. Men must put away childish speaking, seek the truth, and execute judgment. They must follow the words of one of the greatest men of all time, King David, who said, "To all generations I will make known Thy faithfulness with my mouth," and who advised us to speak acceptable, appropriate words for the season (Pss. 89:1; 19:14). Men must speak words of life to their children, spouses, and neighbors. Through prayer and the Word, we have solutions, standards, and convictions in our mouths.

Not only must we speak these words, but we must also live them. We must gather in men's meetings and talk about more than sports and news. We must confess our faults, weaknesses, and fears to one another so we can be healed.

We need to put away childish words and start speaking the truth.

Childish Understanding. Men must put away childish understanding. A childish man falls prey to the domination of his cravings: "I want what I want, when I want, no matter what." This kind of mind is dominated by the current, the "now," the fads.

Every man is responsible to teach his generation the praises of God—his wonders and strengths, and his testimonies and commandments (see Ps. 78). We are to disciple our children so that they touch their own generation with expressions of hope in God.

We need to put away childish understanding and see the world as God sees it.

Childish Thoughts. Men must put away childish thoughts. The self-centered outlook, characterized by lots of "me," "I," and "mine" speech, reflects a lack of restraint and no sense of the relationship between actions and consequences. To be mature, men must understand that we are born dependent and move toward independence, only to discover that we need one another.

We need to put away childish thinking and focus more on others.

A manly outlook says, "I owe this generation what God placed in me, and I can't die until I have left this deposit on earth." David expressed it this way: "Even when I am old and gray, O God, do not forsake me, until I declare Thy strength to this generation, Thy power to all who are to come."[20]

Men must see beyond themselves to invest themselves in this generation. Children spend all they have today, giving no thought to what's ahead. But a good man leaves an inheritance for his children and his children's children.[21] The inheritance is both spiritual and in substance, like David, who made provision for his son Solomon to build the temple.

God created men to serve him. Those who acknowledge Him become the mighty men needed in our day. Following Jesus Christ, they put away childish things so they can speak, understand, and think as men. They have the spirit to pour out wisdom and understanding to their own sons and the sons of others. Some call them a "new breed" of man. I call them men who have rediscovered responsibility and dominion. They know the true meaning of manhood.

Ben Kinchlow is one of the new breed. He writes in the next chapter about having the courage to face reality and make decisions.

I DON'T HAVE TO IF I DON'T WANT TO

by Ben Kinchlow

Imagine this. The Creator of the universe. The Lord God, coming down in the cool of the evening and walking through the garden. The air is heavy with the lush perfumes of ten thousand plants and ripening fruits. The heavy foliage mutes the sounds of a thousand songbirds, and a quietly rippling stream flows out from the garden and is lost in the distance, its passage marked by the accompanying vegetation through the starkly beautiful outworld. And behold "it was very good."

But wait, where is the main reason for his visit? His friend, his designated overseer who is to rule here in God's stead. The voice of God, not loud, yet the garden reverberates with its power, creation holds its breath; the Creator speaks, low, musical, yet falling across every spectrum of sound, irresistible, compelling: "Adam, where are you?"

From his hiding place (hiding from God?) the object of the Creator's visit calls out: "I heard You walking, and I hid because I was naked and afraid." A pause, it seems an eternity, and the sudden gravity in the Creator's tone is frightful indeed. Wanting desperately to cover up but compelled by the voice, Adam confesses. He does what most red-blooded modern Western civilized men do under similar circumstances. He blames his wife and starts a cycle that has continued right up to today. Offer a man a business deal, and often his first response is "Let me talk it over with my wife." Concerned? Compassionate? Seeking her good advice? No. He just wants someone to blame if he agrees and the deal fails. He wants someone else ultimately to be responsible.

When God created Adam, he gave him dominion. That meant God put him in charge. Answerable only to God himself. A free man, but freedom and responsibility can no more be separated than the white from the red in a candy cane. What an awe-inspiring thought. Absolute freedom to make our own choices. So why do we tremble at the thought? Because it makes us responsible for those choices, and people don't want the consequences of their choices. We want the freedom without the consequence. That is not liberty, that is license. Think of it as a modern, pretzel-shaped roller coaster. The terror of an eighty-foot drop and a hurtling upside-down twist, a pause to catch your breath, and *wham!*—through the loop-the-loop. If you're not prepared, the ride takes your breath away.

Lack of Responsibility: The Fuel of Slavery

My ancestors paid the price of men who wanted to exercise dominion and authority without accepting responsibility. Centuries ago, American men wanted other men as their slaves. But they didn't want the car-ing obligations that came with the position. The Bible addresses slave owners: "Masters, provide your slaves with what is right and fair, because you know that you also have a Master in heaven."[1]

Slaveholders who abused their authority lacked the right to quote Scriptures such as, "All who are under the yoke of slavery should consider their masters worthy of full respect"[2] or Ephesians 6:5, which tells us "Slaves, obey your earthly masters with respect and fear" (NIV). I remember the first time I came across that verse. I agreed with everything Paul was saying in the verses right before that. Wives *should* be subject to their husbands. After all, aren't many of the problems in homes today because wives aren't subject to their husbands? Children *should* obey and respect their parents. Fathers *shouldn't* abuse their children. "Right on, Paul," I shouted. "Preach it, brother, preach it."

But when I reached that verse, I nearly choked. *What? Wait a minute!* I read it again. It still said, "Slaves, obey your earthly masters with respect and fear." I snorted, "This is obviously cultural. It's not for today. No way!" Suddenly the apostle had gone from speaking under the anointing of the Holy Spirit to telling my ancestors to be subject to their masters. How could this be?

Then my eyes crawled back up the page. I reread from a new perspective. Scripture always gives us the means to interpret it and principles to resolve conflict. Whenever I don't understand something, I pray and reread the Scriptures, asking God for wisdom. By doing that, I received new insights into such verses as these:

- "Wives, submit to your own husbands, as to the Lord."[3] From a wife's perspective, I saw that she could react with the same indignation I had felt toward the idea of slaves obeying their masters.

- A husband whose wife isn't "acting" the way he feels she should struggles to meet Paul's challenge: "Husbands, love your wives, just as Christ loved the church."[4]
- Children who suffer unreasonable, overbearing, abusive parents would shake their heads to read, "Children, obey your parents in the Lord, for this is right."[5]

When I reached the words about slaves and masters, I wondered what had changed. Why was I cheering "Amen!" one minute and disagreeing with the Bible the next? Why are we suddenly ready to relegate it to a cultural milieu of generations past—as some do or would like to, especially the notion of wives being subject to their husbands? Yet there I was, about to insist, *That's not for today. The Scripture was addressing an issue that was only prevalent in that day. We're almost to the twenty-first century, and these things no longer apply. They're just throwbacks to another time.*

Meditating on it, I realized that what had changed was not the truth, but my position. Scripture addresses principles, not activities. God speaks through truths that transcend time and culture. Without this knowledge, we can easily label entire Bible passages "passé."

The Bible Is Relevant

Now, the Scriptures were addressing me. We weren't talking about abstracts. This was a right-now principle. The same Scripture that tells wives to be subject to their husbands commands husbands to love their wives. Husbands who do that discover their wives don't have to struggle to submit to a selfless, loving man who serves his mate and children with the character of Jesus.

Likewise, a wife's submission to her husband parallels the husband's submission to Christ. When men experience God's sacrificial, disciplined love, they can, in turn, give that love to their families.

With such a mutually beneficial relationship, warm, loving homes become the rule rather than the exception. Wives aren't property or footstools but are equal and valued in the marriage. Children aren't captives but are fully appreciated family participants.

But what about this "slaves subject to their masters" business? As I continued to meditate, the Lord showed me another perspective, one that I believe has long been concealed in the measure God intended. While many have taught this concept, it often comes in a context that obscures the doctrine's meaning and purpose.

What is this issue? Individual responsibility. From *individual responsibility* flow freedom, liberty, and dominion. *Dominion* means our right to make our own decisions and exercise our power of free will over our world. In other words, if Scripture tells slaves to be obedient to their masters and wives to submit to their husbands, it means we have a choice in the matter, and we are responsible for the outcome of our behavior. Why? Because we have dominion, the right to make our own decisions.

This means that *a man can be held in bondage, but he can never be truly enslaved involuntarily*. A man becomes a slave only when he voluntarily submits his free will to another person or condition. For example, the Egyptians held Joseph in captivity and put him to forced labor, but they didn't enslave him. He refused to surrender his free will. The Babylonians took many Israelites captive. But Daniel, Shadrach, Meschach, and Abednego refused to become slaves.

▲ ▲ ▲ ▲ ▲

A man becomes a slave only when he voluntarily submits his free will to another person or condition.

▼ ▼ ▼ ▼ ▼

Since you can only be enslaved willingly, consider this truth in your relationship to Jesus Christ: Don't just acknowledge him as Savior—though that's a necessary step for salvation—but also as Lord. The Bible tells us, "No one can say, 'Jesus is Lord,' except by the Holy Spirit."[6] Calling him "Lord" implies the voluntary surrender of your free will to him.

There are not many better examples than Paul, who wrote, "Rejoice in the Lord always; again I will say, rejoice!"[7] Though he recognized Caesar's authority over him, Paul called himself a "bond servant" of Christ. It didn't matter that the greatest secular power in existence had imprisoned him—he was already a slave of Jesus Christ. Though chained to a Roman soldier, his spirit and mind were not captive except to the Lord.

He went on to say, "I know how to get along with humble means, and I also know how to live in prosperity; in any and every circumstance I have learned the secret of being filled and going hungry, both of having abundance and suffering need. I can do all things through Him who strengthens me."[8] He wrote that from a jail cell!

God made each of us free moral agents, empowered with choice and dominion. Given that freedom, we must refuse to surrender our liberty to anyone except Christ. But with this dominion comes *individual responsibility*.

Acting irresponsibly is not liberty but license. This foolishness is seen everywhere today. We have so blurred the distinction between the liberty of freedom and the license of irresponsibility that they are indistinguishable. We love our freedom but hate responsibility. Consequently, men want to exercise dominion but without taking any responsibility.

The power to choose must bow to the Source of that power. That's why Jesus told his disciples, "All authority has been given to Me in heaven and on earth. Go therefore. . . ."[9] Put another way, He was saying, "You are empowered to proceed as authorized, designated bearers of my authority."

Even Jesus operated under his Father's authority. The Gospel of Matthew tells a story about a Roman centurion who came to Jesus, seeking healing for one of his servants. Jesus offered to go to the Roman's home.

> **God made each of us free moral agents, empowered with choice and dominion. With this dominion comes individual responsibility.**

The centurion replied that he wasn't worthy. "But only speak a word, and my servant will be healed,"[10] he said, explaining that he was a man under authority, and that when he gave orders, they were carried out. In recognizing that Jesus, too, operated under authority, the centurion gained Christ's approval. In that hour, his servant was healed.

We again see Christ exercising his Father's authority in the Crucifixion account. Taken captive by the mob that wanted to put him to death, Jesus said, "Do you think that I cannot appeal to My Father, and He will at once put at My disposal more than twelve legions of angels?."[11] When he stood before Pontius Pilate, the human authority with the power to release him, he said, "You would have no authority over Me, unless it had been given you from above."[12]

Reaping What We've Sown

All husbands, fathers, wives, mothers, singles, and young children have the freedom to act. But they also must accept responsibility for their actions. Failure to do so leads to chaos. And chaos is exactly what we're facing as we come into the potential "death grip" of a generation raised with little or no sense of responsibility for its actions.

Decades ago, we planted the seeds of today's destruction. Anyone who lived through the 1960s recognizes the sayings that grew out of it: "If it feels good, do it." "Tune in, turn on, drop out." "Whatever turns you on." "Ethics depend on the situation." Now each year, for example, the overwhelming majority of abortions done in the United States are the result of liberty without responsibility. We want the freedom to engage in extramarital sexual activities, but we don't want the responsibilities that go with our "free sex."

Take the outbreaks of syphilis and gonorrhea in the 1950s and 1960s. We greeted penicillin shots and condoms with joy because they freed us from the fear of disease. Instead of worrying about the consequences of social disease or changing our behavior, we just "got a shot." Our solutions did nothing to encourage morality but enabled us to continue on the same foolish path.

In the 1990s, AIDS has dramatically changed the consequences, but we still see no shift toward morality. Our society tells people (particularly teens), "You have the freedom to act irresponsibly. But use a condom." In other words, if it feels good, do it . . . but safely.

The Terror of Freedom

The good news—and the bad news—is that God gives us the ability to act independently of Him. *"I don't have to if I don't want to"* is more than the cry of a petulant child. It's a clear statement of our position as men made in the image of God and given dominion over the earth.

The same wondrous, terrifying feeling comes with yielding to the lordship of Christ. We make decisions knowing we are firmly fastened to him who promised, "I will never leave you nor forsake you."[13] He will not let us go. And with that confidence, we have the freedom to submit our wills to his, living to please him and accepting responsibility for the choices we make along the way.

Fasten your seat belt. You're on the road to true manhood, and with help from the brothers in the next two chapters, you'll be heading there fast.

Part Two

MAN, WOMAN, CHILD

Love never fails.

1 Corinthians 13:8

◀ 5 ▶

DO WE NEED A WOMEN'S MOVEMENT?

by A. R. Bernard

In the early 1950s, a nineteen-year-old sprinter's fame spread throughout Panama, Venezuela, and the rest of Central and South America. In the prime of her career, she captured gold and silver medals in the 400-meter and other Olympic races and appeared destined for even greater triumphs. Tuskegee Institute in Alabama offered her a scholarship, and a promise to fly her to America left her brimming with bright goals and dreams.

Across from the track where she practiced, a restaurant owner watched her each day. Gradually, this older man won her affections. Innocent, flattered by the attentions of a mature male, and lured by his promises of lasting togetherness, she gave in to his advances. Soon she was pregnant. In that era, unwed pregnancy brought scandal in the local athletic community and among all who read about it across the nation.

When she gave birth, the young woman lost both her scholarship and her place on the track team. Yet, she didn't mind that much. Someone still loved her—or so she thought. After her release from the maternity ward, the young woman brought her son to his father, hoping he would bless the infant with his name. Instead, the man rejected the baby and the woman, refusing even to accept financial responsibility for the boy's upbringing. Now she had lost everything. This final blow was the cruelest.

Devastated and bitter, she prayed that one day this baby would grow up, somehow pick up where she had left off, and contribute to society. Though mother and son became close friends as he matured, she still struggled with life. She married a few times, but those unions crumbled. She had never resolved the pain caused by her son's father.

The child never knew his dad. At first he was too young to understand what had happened, but when he grew old enough, his father had died. His mother's faint hope that somehow the two would come together dissolved. In spite of her despair, she fought, manipulated, and struggled to survive, the way many women do, so that her boy would have an opportunity to succeed.

I know the details of this story so intimately because I am that child. My father thought only in terms of the present moment. He never realized that when a man looks at a woman, he gazes at destiny, something much greater than himself. When a man plays with and manipulates a woman, forcing her into corners of compromise, he tampers with the future of the world.

Throughout history men have tended to be casual with their words. They continually make promises to women and then break them, especially husbands with their wives. This creates insecurity in women. They don't know whether they can trust men or not. In spite of planting these seeds of doubt, men become hostile when women question their commitment and angry at the challenge to their integrity. Men fail to realize that they are themselves responsible for the very insecurity they've sown.

Revolutionary Change

A valuable principle taught by the Christian Men's Network is that if change does not come voluntarily from the top, it will take place from the bottom through revolution. The oppression of women had gone on worldwide for centuries. But thanks to the free voice women had in the United States, they vowed to create a revolution. Uniting their efforts, they demanded legislation to get the respect and appreciation they should have received automatically from men.

Yet, this caused problems. Any truth taken to the extreme can produce error. The extremes of women's liberation produced a movement of lesbianism, the promotion of homosexuality, and a damaging liberality in our nation's morals. Interestingly, many women who once identified with the feminist movement have reconsidered their approach. Why? Because they became frustrated when they couldn't find the man they were looking for within themselves.

In March 1994, *U.S. News & World Report* featured a cover story titled "The War Against Women." It recalled the band of militant women who, twenty-five years before, had picketed the Miss America pageant in Atlantic City. Tossing bras, girdles, and other paraphernalia into heaps, they set fire to them. The blaze became a symbol. The "bra burners" stood at the forefront of this new women's liberation movement.[1]

The movement spread worldwide, yet the inequities persisted. A United Nations report in 1980 summed up the problems women still faced at that time. Though they made up half the world's population, they did two-thirds of the work. For their wages, they received one-tenth of the world's income. They owned a mere one-hundredth of the world's property.[2]

However, American women who feel trampled can look at two communist nations to see how bad it can get. When the Soviet Union collapsed in 1991, women found themselves tossed into lesser jobs in the workplace. Often they learned that part of their job description included sleeping with the boss. Likewise, though China's economy has grown at a double-digit clip in recent years, most workers in the sweatshops are women. Beijing has ranked women's health, employment, and educational needs below the goal of keeping birth rates low. Even worse, in China, India, and many other countries where sons are still more highly valued than daughters, medical technology forced on women makes it easier than ever to dispose of unwanted baby girls. Abortion is not necessarily "pro-choice."

We can understand the world's problems and its mistreatment of women through a biblical perspective. Go back to the beginning of human history. God put Adam to sleep and took from him the elements to create Eve. Whatever he took out of Adam to make Eve, he never replaced. Thus, Adam could not be Eve, and Eve could not be Adam.

God made a clear separation between the two sexes, declaring them to be male and female. That's why, when a woman attempts to be a man, she often exaggerates male characteristics. It's not natural to her. So it is, too, with those homosexual males who determine to act like women. They exaggerate a woman's mannerisms and become more effeminate than females.

Despite the monumental battle waged by revolutionary feminists, "liberated" women cannot accomplish what they set out to do. The oppression of women and other ills that plague our nation and world will continue to exist unless there's a change in men. Women's liberation will never succeed because it is men who must change.

That's why I praise God for the men's movement and those like Ed Cole who are meeting the challenge to change men's lives. Because of his teaching, I placed an emphasis on strong men in our church. As a result, 52 percent of Christian Life Centre's membership is men, and our women love it. The more men conform to the image of Christ, the freer women become.

Man Brought Sin

The Bible says, "Therefore, just as through one man sin entered into the world, and death through sin, and so death spread to all men, because all sinned."[3] Sin came through one man, not one woman. Once I pointed this out, and a man got upset, saying, "Well, that's not talking about man, *per se*, the male gender. It's talking about humankind."

No, I don't believe you can stretch the term that way. At its heart, the Greek root means "man." There was one man and one woman, and sin came through the man. Why else, when God came looking for the two people in the Garden of Eden after they had sinned, did he call to Adam and say, "Where are you?"[4]

This passage reflects the reason things go wrong in a home, community, nation, and world: something has gone wrong with the men. Sin, sickness, and oppression enter a society through men. That's why we men have such an awesome responsibility. Our actions decide the world's fate.

When Eve ate the forbidden fruit, the Bible says she then gave it to her husband, who was with her.[5] In other words, he observed what happened—*and ate the fruit anyway!* Now, the Bible doesn't say they ate simultaneously. Immediately after Eve's mistake, Adam was still righteous and in fellowship with God. He had the opportunity to do what the Bible says the husband should do, which is to be the savior of her body—literally, to die for her if necessary.[6] Adam could have redeemed Eve.

> **Men's greatest failings are not in what we do, but in what we don't do.**

Not only did God call to Adam first, but he also spoke to him first, asking how he knew he was naked and then asking if Adam had eaten of the forbidden fruit.[7] Adam was responsible. His greatest sin was not what he did but what he didn't do. So it is with men today: Men's greatest failings are not in what we do but in what we don't do.

When we men fail to assume our responsibilities and to take righteous action, we incite women to assume a role for which they weren't designed. It is shameful to a man if a woman lowers her standards and adopts the mentality of a survivalist. When a woman does that, it's generally because a man in her life didn't take the responsibility for her that belonged to him.

The women's liberation movement and the state of some women who have stooped to survive in the world are tied to men's failure to be responsible.

There are millions of such women in our society who have not resolved painful issues and bear deep-seated scars. But men like to push them into the corner where they don't have to deal with them.

When we men fail to assume our responsibilities and take righteous actions, we incite women to assume a role for which they weren't designed.

My wife, Karen, gave me some insight into this issue during one of our past struggles to communicate. "Well, why don't you tell me the truth?" I fumed once, to which she shot back, "You're not ready for the truth."

At first I thought, *Whoa, what did I do?* But as we worked through the problem, I saw how blind men can be. We fail to grasp the effects we have on women, the results of our failure to demonstrate integrity, consistency, decisiveness, and strength. When women stoop to trickery or manipulation to get us men to do what we're supposed to do anyway, they depart from their God-designed pattern.

Unfortunately, the pattern of men blaming their actions on others goes all the way back to Adam. So does refusal to accept responsibility for our actions. Look at Judah, the father of the tribe that gave birth to Jesus. This is a man who played a crucial role in the history of the world, and his life serves as a lesson to men of all generations.

Judah and Tamar

In the midst of the story of Joseph's sale into slavery, the Bible detours to tell us about Judah leaving his brothers to marry a Canaanite woman. They had three sons, Er, Onan, and Shelah. When Er grew up, Judah found a wife for him named Tamar. Quickly, though, Er departed from the scene because he "was evil in the sight of the LORD, so the LORD took his life."[8]

For Tamar, things got worse. Given by the Lord through Moses, Hebrew law dictated that when a man died with no children, his brother was to marry his dead brother's wife and raise an heir so the dead brother's name would live on. Instead, however, Onan rebelled. Knowing that the resulting child wouldn't be his, when he had intercourse with Tamar, he spilled his seed on the ground. God's remedy? "He took his life also."[9]

Now Judah was getting a little nervous. He only had three sons, and the two who were married to this woman were gone. Nevertheless, he made a promise to Tamar, telling her to remain a widow in her father's house until the third son, Shelah, grew to manhood. Yet in his heart, he sent her away fearing "that he too may die like his brothers."[10]

The problem here lay with Judah passing the buck. After Onan died in his rebellion, Judah had a responsibility to be a covering over Tamar until another covering could be presented. But instead of meeting the challenge head-on, he first stalled for time and then forgot his promise. Sound familiar?

The full story of Judah's cowardice continued to unfold. When his wife died, Judah sought comfort, then went off to shear his sheep. Tamar heard about it, took off her widow's garments, covered herself with a veil, and waited in the countryside, "for she saw that Shelah had grown up, and she had not been given to him as a wife."[11]

Tamar had taken extreme action. When a woman veiled her face, it was because she didn't want to reveal her identity. Usually, it meant she was a prostitute. That's what Judah believed when he saw her: "So he turned aside to her by the road, and said, 'Here now, let me come in to you'; for he did not know that she was his daughter-in-law."[12]

Her response was direct: "What will you give me, that you may come in to me?" In other words, she didn't trust this man. With good reason! He had sown the seeds of insecurity through his past failures. Though he promised to send her a young goat from his flock, she demanded a pledge, so he gave her his signet, cord, and staff.

Tamar was smart. She knew she might need those personal objects later. Because of Judah's irresponsible behavior, Tamar became a mastermind at plotting and scheming. If he denied his act later, she held ironclad proof that he had propositioned her.

Once the deed was complete, Tamar put her widow's clothes back on, having to change personalities again to maintain her dignity. Apparently, she had managed to keep on her veil and keep hidden her identity.

Finally, Judah kept a promise. He sent a young goat to the harlot, hoping to get back the tokens of his pledge (and probably this was the only reason he kept his word). Yet the woman was nowhere to be found.

That reminds me of some men today. They won't blink an eye when paying for a prostitute's favors, but they complain bitterly about supporting their wives and children.

Three months later, when word came to Judah that his daughter-in-law was pregnant, his response was direct: "Bring her out and let her be burned!"[13] Finally, he thought, his responsibility was over. Now he could get rid of this embarrassment without facing the consequences of his actions.

Instead, however, he faced a surprise. Tamar said she would reveal the father of her child, and she brought out Judah's signet, cord, and staff. Confronted with the truth, he confessed, "'She is more righteous than I, inasmuch as I did not give her to my son Shelah.' And he did not have relations with her again."[14]

Taking Responsibility

When Judah acted irresponsibly and Tamar manipulated him, neither of them realized their involvement in something much greater than themselves. God was severe with Er and Onan because of Tamar's place in the genealogy of Christ. She held the future within her. She had to conceive to pass on the seed that would endure through forty-two generations.

Likewise, when men fail to understand the responsibility God places on them, they fail to realize they're a part of something much greater than themselves. Through our sins of omission, we force women to compromise their virtues, lower their standards, and even sacrifice their integrity.

Only when men assume their rightful responsibilities will the world find the solutions it so desperately seeks.

So how will things change? Never as a result of a women's liberation movement or bra burning. Only when men assume their rightful responsibilities will the world find the solutions it so desperately seeks. A movement of men becoming transformed into the image of Jesus Christ will produce exemplary role models of decisiveness and righteousness.

This is why we now see a great move in men's ministry, because men are submitting themselves to the lordship of Jesus Christ. The answer to changing society comes from men completing their true manhood and establishing families under God's direction.

No, we don't need a women's liberation movement but a men's responsibility movement. The only way to change society corporately is to change men individually.

To change may sound difficult, but we can all do it. You can do it. You can see the destiny held by the women around you and respect them for it. And you can see how by doing so, you are part of something greater than yourself.

Mike Singletary is one man who has overcome a broken family background, as well as the temptations and pitfalls of fame and money as a football player, to take on the responsibility of his wife and children. As spoiled as many of our professional athletes are today, Mike's story in the next chapter gives a strong example of what a real man is when he overcomes circumstances to fulfill his God-given responsibilities in the home.

The only way to change society corporately is to change men individually.

MAN OF THE WORLD, MAN OF THE HOUSE

by Mike Singletary

Kim and I sat across from each other on the floor of a tropical beach bungalow during what should have been a dream vacation. Instead of rest and recreation, though, I faced the greatest test of my manhood. In the next few minutes, I'd either tell Kim the truth about myself and stand as a man, or I would slink off like a wimp. A giant wall of guilt and fear stood between me and my wife and between me and my manhood.

I had always looked manly enough. I spent twelve years in the National Football League as one of the smallest linebackers in the professional game—and one of the few players with a hearing impairment. But I overcame my physical limitations with hard work and an insatiable desire to know everything about my opponent. Opposing coaches complained that I knew their plays better than their own players did. It paid off. I led the defense on a Chicago Bears Super Bowl team, took down opponents twice my size, and earned Pro Bowl honors year after year.

During my glory years, I married my college sweetheart. It no doubt appeared to everyone, including Kim, that we had everything going for us—not only fame and fortune on this earth, but also a shared Christian faith, with an eternity of God's love ahead of us.

If you forgive someone, you release that sin out of your life. But if you refuse to forgive, you bind that sin to yourself and end up repeating it, or living with the guilt, shame, hurt, bitterness, and anger it brings.

But after marrying Kim, problems from deep within me came out. I was angry and withdrawn much of the time. At first I did what every guy probably does—blamed her. Then I realized she was just responding to me. I was the one with problems, part of which stemmed from the guilt of cheating on her throughout our engagement. I had worked through some things, but now it was time to face the truth. Through me, guilt, hurt, and bitterness were killing our marriage.

As the tenth child of a broken home, raised mostly by a single mother, I experienced my first great breakthrough as a man by reconciling with my dad. My parents divorced when my father left us for another woman, and I had never forgiven him for that.

Jesus said that if we forgive the sins of anyone, they are forgiven. But if we retain the sins of anyone, they are retained.[1] That means that if you forgive someone, you release that sin out of your life. But if you refuse to forgive, you bind that sin to yourself and end up repeating it or living with the guilt, shame, hurt, bitterness, and anger it brings. Before I forgave my dad, I was actually binding his sin to myself and dragging old resentments and habits into my marriage. No wonder I made life so hellish for Kim.

I finally brought myself to call Dad and talk to him about how he'd left us. Although I was angry, reliving all the hurt of my childhood, we talked like men. After I unloaded on him, he told me things I'd never known or thought of before. I could see how people get pushed into situations they never intended. It didn't make him right, just human. By the end of the call, we were both crying and making up. I forgave him, and he forgave me, too, for holding it against him all those years.

Since then, I've heard of men writing letters to a deceased father, just to get those feelings off their chests and to forgive their dads so they could live without the past sins bothering them. Whatever it takes, it's worth it.

Forgiving Dad was like a rite of passage into manhood. I always wanted to be a man. Ever since I was five years old, going to construction sites with Dad, I wanted to be "the boss" one day. To be in control of my own destiny. To provide for a family of my own.

I was brought into the world even though the doctors told Mama she should abort me because of illness. I went through all the aches and pains of childhood as a sickly kid with bad hearing. But I clung to my goal—to be a man. I lived on that dream, thrived on it, excelling in everything I did so I could become the man I saw in my mind's eye.

Mama emphasized education, so I studied hard and promised to try for a scholarship—not even knowing what a scholarship was other than something to be proud of. Education wasn't easy for me, but I saw it as both a way out of the ghetto and a means of controlling my own destiny. To get through college, I dogged professors night and day to help me. I was so determined to know everything that I sometimes wore them out. One of them left a note on his door once that said, "Not today, Mike." Others avoided me in more subtle ways. But mostly they stood by me and helped.

I graduated with an earned degree instead of a piece of paper they gave me for my football ability. And it paid off quickly. Early in my football career, I stopped hiring agents. I found I could do their work myself with as much success—and without sharing my earnings.

But after all I had overcome in my life, what was between me and Kim was the hardest obstacle ever to stand in the way of my goal—real manhood. I had to put into practice what I'd read in the Bible, to love my wife as Christ loves the church. Putting my love for my wife before my love for myself was harder than any injury, any workout, any coach's angry words, or any final exam I'd ever suffered. Perhaps because of my high profile, or the depth of friendship Kim and I had as a foundation for our marriage, I did not feel right simply repenting in private without truly reconciling my past with my wife. Other men have left the past behind and spared their wives the grief of knowing the truth. But as I prayed and struggled to find peace within, I knew God was requiring that I do the hardest thing I'd ever done: Tell the truth.

By telling Kim the truth about the man she married, I risked my marriage or, at the very least, all the respect and trust she had for me, which could take years to rebuild. I honestly didn't know what I would gain from my confession, because until then I didn't even know what a happy marriage was. All I knew was that to become a real man, I had to die to my pride and become vulnerable to my wife.

Like straining to bench-press a great weight, I labored with the words, forcing myself to make them come out. I finally choked out about how I cheated on her while we were dating; about why I went away for long periods "to be alone"; about why, now that we were married, I had rejected her by withdrawing from her love.

Her reaction was worse than anything I'd expected. She didn't fly at me, yelling, throwing things, or cursing. Instead, she sat dazed, so hurt she was numb, until slowly the tears began to come. They lasted for days.

What I'd been facing was horrible and had left me sleepless many nights, but this was even worse. All I could do was think, *What have I done to the woman God entrusted to me?* Day after day, she asked questions, and I filled in all the gaps: all the lies I'd told her; all the women I'd seen; all the people who knew but didn't say anything to her.

Kim was so deeply hurt and humiliated that I didn't know if our marriage could survive. Now that I had a clean slate, I wanted our marriage to work more than anything, but it seemed in worse shape than ever. Yet strangely, for reasons I was still learning, my prayer life was invigorated. For the first time, I could go before the Father boldly and intercede for my wife and marriage.

The Bible says that if husbands don't treat their wives as joint-heirs in Christ, their prayers won't get ready answers.[2] I experienced this firsthand. Where before I had struggled to pray, to tell God my deepest feelings, now I was pouring my heart out to him daily with full confidence that he was not only hearing, but also answering. I felt free for the first time. I was no longer living a double life. I was being exactly who I am—inside and out—without wearing a mask, without depending on my reputation, without the short temper that had characterized me before. With nothing to hide, there was nothing to be angry about anymore. I could honestly say, "I am who I am."

If husbands don't treat their wives as joint heirs in Christ, their prayers won't get ready answers.

That gave me the faith to stand strong while Kim and our marriage recovered. Kim's hurt slowly subsided, and her trust in me began to grow once again. As she healed, our marriage was transformed into what marriages are supposed to be. There were no more walls between us. For the first time, she really knew the man she married. Now that she knew, and now that I had nothing left to be ashamed of, I learned to love in a way I'd never known.

When God helped me deal with my sin, first with my father, then with my wife, I began to experience for the first time what it really meant to have Christ in my heart. Sure, I had been a Christian. But I never fully experienced the Lord within me because I wasn't open to his truth, forgiveness, grace, or love.

I'm convinced that the women's movement came about because our society didn't have enough real men. And only real men can make it in this world. For me, with all the fame and accolades, I was still miserable. It took more than fame and fortune to make me feel like a man. A hundred-dollar bill in my wallet didn't do it.

Women don't have much to look forward to if the men around them only talk about how much money they have, what kind of car they drive, or how good they are in bed. That's not manhood. That's a practiced avoidance of the real issues of life.

When it comes to women, men tend to take the Scriptures and go too far. They take the biblical principle of "headship" and "leadership" and turn it into dictatorship and superiority. Man's leadership is to be patterned after Jesus—leadership through serving and loving. Jesus said that to be a leader, you have to be the servant of all.[3] The husband is supposed to love his wife as Christ loves the church.[4]

Many men think the passage about women submitting to men gives them the right to subject their wives to servanthood.[5] In reality, the whole passage implies that if a man loves his wife in a godly, selfless, servantlike way, she will *want* to submit to his leadership. When men exercise their authority in the way it's outlined in the Bible, women don't resent it.

Women who are loved as Christ loves find their needs met, find outlets for their gifts and talents, and find themselves appreciated.

In business, you quickly learn about appreciation and depreciation. Things that appreciate increase in value. What depreciates decreases in value.[6] This is more than a lesson in finance—it's a lesson in women. Appreciate your wife, and she'll increase in value—to you as well as to herself. Cut her down, treat her like a slave, and she'll quickly depreciate—to you and to herself.

I've heard that people who have quit smoking are the hardest on smokers. That's how I feel about marriage. For me, now that God has changed my relationship with my wife, I find it disgusting and embarrassing to be around men who tell their wives or girlfriends what to do, where to stand or sit, to shut up, to go over there, or to leave them alone.

> **Appreciate your wife, and she'll increase in value. Cut her down, treat her like a slave, and she'll quickly depreciate—to you and to herself.**

Like many men, I used the word *love* so carelessly, without any understanding. To use the word properly, a man must have a degree of maturity. He must have some character, some sense of responsibility, and then he must be willing to put love into action.

Kim and I had one of my teenage nieces living with our family. I told her not to believe any guy who says "I love you" unless he has corresponding actions. I told her to respond to a guy who proclaims his love by saying, "The greatest act of love ever was Jesus Christ giving his life for me. Is that what you're prepared to do?"

A typical man mistakenly believes that what would make him happy is a gorgeous wife who takes care of his needs on demand, makes him proud, and serves him. But that isn't God's kind of love. His love is _sacrificial, redemptive, and selfless._

For everything good God has created, there's a cheap counterfeit. The counterfeit of love is lust. Lust desires to benefit self even at the expense of others, because lust desires to get. Love desires to benefit others even at the expense of self, because love desires to give.[7]

In the first book of Corinthians is a chapter known as the "love chapter." It's short, but it spells out what true love is. Once I broke through the barriers of guilt and fear that hindered my manhood, love became the theme of my life, my anthem, my pledge. Learning to love as God loves—_sacrificially, redemptively, and selflessly_—has revolutionized my marriage and my relationship with each of my kids. The passage says in part:

> _Love is kind and patient,_
> _never jealous, boastful, proud, or rude._
> _Love isn't selfish or quick tempered._
> _It doesn't keep a record of wrongs that others do._
> _Love rejoices in the truth, but not in evil._
> _Love is always supportive, loyal, hopeful, and trusting._
> _Love never fails!_[8]

Loving with God's kind of love means that you can insert your name wherever it says "love" and read it:

"[Mike] is kind and patient. . . ." What a way to measure your manhood!

This is the kind of love we need in the black community today. Too many of my black brothers are bailing out on their families, or worse, never owning up to their responsibilities. In many ways, we've forgotten our roots. We remember slavery, the ruthless oppression, the anger and despair. But we've forgotten the important things, like how closely we used to work with our wives. That was part of the reason we were able to hold our families together and withstand the worst of circumstances.

We don't often see unconditional love in our marriages anymore—working for each other's benefit sacrificially, loving each other unselfishly. For many years I thought the examples I saw around me were how life was supposed to be, full of selfishness, anger, and regret. Then I read the Bible and found out that my wife and I were to serve each other in love. I am to help her, and she is to help me.

Love is the road to greatness, and it's the final reward as well.

If we would be loving husbands to our wives and loving fathers to our children, instead of getting tied up and sidetracked in selfish agendas, we would strengthen our communities. We would be able to keep our young people out of prison and get our people off government assistance. By learning to love as God loves, we can break the curse of centuries.

I always aspired to great things in my Christian walk, but I never understood what love was until that moment of truth with Kim. Once I understood love, embraced it, and applied myself to it, love became both the beginning and the end for me. Love is the road to greatness, and it's the final reward as well.

Get on with your manhood. Learn how to forgive your parents, your teachers, your wife—yourself. Then let the love of God surge through you. Love God. Love others. Love yourself. And *show* your love through unselfish leadership. You may never make it to the Pro Bowl, but you can be an All-Star, one of God's shining examples of manhood.

In the next few chapters, a couple of great men are going to help you apply what you've been reading about. So keep your cleats on. You're just starting to tackle your dream—real manhood.

Part Three

GETTING STARTED

My servants will be called by another name.

Isaiah 65:15

CHANGE YOUR NAME

by Eddie Long

Though decades have passed, the taunts and head slaps remain burned in my memory. *Whap!* came the flick of the hand that felt like a shovel smacking my brain. But the words stung more painfully, exploding into my spirit like rockets and inflicting gaping emotional wounds.

"Look, brothers, it's Eddie Lee Longhead!"

"Hey, what happened to yo' hair?"

"Is that yo' head, man, or is that a hunchback sittin' up there?"

For years I lugged around that hated name. Not Eddie Long. I was Eddie Lee Longhead, the goofball nobody wanted around. Whenever they chose sides for school-yard games, yours truly was always the last one picked. And then I was taken only because they had no choice: "We gotta take Longhead . . . uh-oh!" I didn't have a girl-friend until I turned sixteen because I never thought a female would want anything to do with me.

I was also "secondhand Eddie," the boy who never wore new clothes. My father was a preacher with four sons. Standing third in line guaranteed me plenty of hand-me-downs.

I'll never forget Easter, when all my buddies got new clothes. In our house, my oldest brother donned a new suit and passed along his older ones. When they got to me, they always looked crooked, ill-fitting, and shiny, but everyone marveled, "Oh, that looks good. Yeah, that looks good!" And I never dared say otherwise.

With shoes, I didn't fare any better. Today everyone talks about Reeboks and Air Jordans, but in my day, the only kind of basketball sneakers to own were Converse. They cost nine bucks. Yet my senior year of high school arrived before I ever slapped on a pair of "Cons." Until then, my feet always settled for canvas collapsible, dime-store specials known as Jeeps.

The worst part of life, though, came from our Saturday night barbering. Before church day, my father gave each of us skin haircuts, which nobody else wore in the 1960s. The "Michael Jordan look" might seem cool now, but it wasn't back then when my bald profile—complete with a strange bump on the back of my noggin—stirred up howls of laughter.

What made me even madder was the lack of moral support. When Daddy wasn't preaching, he was out working on his business. My brothers were busy with their own problems, and friends were few and far between. I hated Valentine's Day because everyone got a valentine except me. Everybody received invitations to birthday parties, but somehow, mine never got delivered.

Those childhood images followed me into my mid-thirties, dogging me like a bloodhound after a scared rabbit. Even as an adult, when I walked down the street and saw someone coming, I crossed over to the other side. I wasn't afraid; I just didn't want to look others in the eye. Not me. Not secondhand Eddie Lee Longhead. I was living up to my name.

Who Named You?

Who named you? Was it your mama who said, "You ain't never going to be no better than your daddy"? Or did your father shake his head as he declared, "You'll never get a job"? Maybe your classmates jeered, "You? You'll never get to college." It could have been a friend who wanted someone else to drown in his misery and moaned, "We'll never be nothin', man, nothin'."

> *Somebody gave you a name, and you won't give it up, even though it's ruining you. It's time to let go!*

What's your name? Who set you up for failure? Who limited your potential? Most important, if you're *way down there*, why? Did you know that God wants you far above the world's petty frustrations?

If throughout your life you have never known victory, if you don't have any peace in your home, and if your marriage hangs by threads, you may be clinging to ancient history. Somebody gave you a name, and you won't give it up, even though it's ruining you. It's time to let go!

The best example of a man in need of a new name comes from the Bible. His name was Jacob.

Jacob spent the night alone.

A man came and fought with Jacob until just before daybreak. When the man saw that he could not win, he struck Jacob on the hip and threw it out of joint. They kept on wrestling until the man said, "Let go of me! It's almost daylight."

"You can't go until you bless me," Jacob replied.

Then the man asked, "What is your name?"

"Jacob," he answered.

The man said, "Your name will no longer be Jacob. You have wrestled with God and with men, and you have won. That's why your name will be Israel."[1]

A great and glorious miracle happened for Jacob that night. At the end of it, Jacob became a new man—Israel. But the best part of the story is that God will do the same for you. The Bible says Christ is the same yesterday, today, and forever.[2] He's ready to change your name today.

"Well, so what?" you ask. "So someone gets a new name. What kind of big deal is that? Where's his new house? How 'bout a hot new camel to help him wheel around the desert? His harem didn't expand. He's not expecting any more children, is he? I don't see any prosperity settling on this cat."

But Jacob's new name was a *monumental blessing*. Jacob meant "supplanter," "deceiver," and "trickster," and until then, that described him very well. In all his dealings, he proved clever and conniving, especially when he tricked his brother out of his birthright. As the oldest son, Esau's position carried a double portion of his father's inheritance and his father's strongest blessing. But Jacob, the younger brother, deceived their father into pronouncing the blessing over him instead.

Jacob became "Israel," meaning "He strives with God (and prevails)." The weak, human deceiver vanished. In his place came a godly legend whose name lives on today.

Who named Jacob? His parents. Who gave him a new name? God.

Who named you? Do you want to know what God's name is for you? Then you must be willing to wrestle with the Almighty with as much determination and expectation as Jacob. You will never change until you find yourself in direct conflict with him. When you face confrontation with God, I guarantee that He won't change, but you will.

In that all-night wrestling match, Jacob came face-to-face with something he couldn't stand: the truth. When he got a good picture of who he was and what he was, he knew he needed God. Jacob cried from his heart, "You've got to bless me, because I'm tired of what I am."

Before he surrendered, Jacob hit bottom. Forced to depart from his father-in-law Laban's home, he neared his brother's domain. Because of his past deception and Esau's vow to get revenge, Jacob feared for his life. First he sent word that he had returned from serving Laban and had all kinds of oxen, donkeys, flocks, and servants, hoping that would appease Esau. Instead, however, messengers returned to say that his brother was on the way with four hundred men. Jacob quickly divided his people and possessions into two camps so at least one could escape if Esau attacked the other.

Jacob was just like you in many ways. He didn't have only one problem, he had two: his most serious problem was that he had already figured out how to solve his other problem. Whenever you go around trying to come up with solutions apart from God, you'll make your problem worse than it was in the beginning.

Finally, after Jacob prayed fervently to be delivered from Esau's hand, he sent his wives, female servants, and eleven children over a stream and stayed behind to go one-on-one with the Lord. His plans had frittered away. Everyone had left him. He had nothing left on which he could rely. And in the silence, God met him.

▲ ▲ ▲ ▲ ▲

Take one night, just one night, to meet God, and He will change your life.

▼ ▼ ▼ ▼ ▼

One-Night Stand

The one-night stand. That term has become common over the past thirty years as our society has followed the foolish ethic of "free love." Sometimes men add another meaning, using it to describe their never-ending poker party, dice game, or beer bash.

The sad thing is, when men like that accept Christ as their Savior and leave those ways behind, they never stay up all night again. "Don't do that no more," they say, but they're missing out on something. Not a hangover, for sure. But why won't they stay up all night to meet with God? They stayed awake with their old drinking buddies, those guys who were taking them down the drain—so why not stay up with God?

Take one night, just one night, to meet God, and he will change your life. Jacob didn't necessarily want to do that, but his plans had failed him, and he had run out of other options. The Lord isolated him where He could speak to him. If you'll seek a place of quiet, where you can be alone, God will speak to you too.

If you're like most men, you don't want to be completely alone. You enjoy being around crowds or with plenty of noise. When you're alone, you turn up the TV or turn on the stereo. You have to have something going, because whenever you face silence, certain thoughts and convictions jump up at you. Not pretty, are they?

But there in the quiet, God can deal with you and show you the mistakes, sins, and rebellion that keep you from fulfilling his call on your life. Those are the things that hold you captive. There's nothing more miserable than to profess Jesus as your Savior and say you walk in holiness, yet to know deep down you're not living that way.

Don't kid yourself; the Lord knows what sins are in your life. Still, you wrestle with them and try to get rid of them, and finally you reach the point that I did. I misinterpreted Paul's second letter to the Corinthians, where he talked about his thorn in the flesh, and reasoned, *Well, I might be like Paul. This is just my thorn.*[3] Maybe you're thinking, *Well, since it's not gone, maybe this is just the way I am. I'm supposed to live with this problem.*

Let me tell you emphatically: No, you're not! God wants to burn that sin out of you. Before Jacob got his new name, something else took place. As Jacob wrestled, God threw his hip out of joint. It was a physical sign of an internal work. In that night, God changed Jacob's character and attitude so that Jacob became worthy of bearing his new name.

When you get alone with your Creator, you may learn more about the source of your dilemma. One problem many Christians have is their failure to understand that they can face conviction or condemnation from three sources—man, Satan, and God. If God is troubling you, you can sit there all day and declare, "I bind you, Satan," and it won't help.

If you wake up in the middle of the night or have problems sleeping, it may be that God wants to talk to you. Listen. You may hear him say, *I'm not going to let you rest. I want to spend the night with you. I don't want you getting comfortable. I'm not going to let you keep going the same direction and enjoying it. I want your attention.*

That's what happened when the prophet Samuel was a boy. Everyone was sleeping when somebody called him. Since he lived with the high priest Eli, Samuel naturally ran to him and asked, "Did you call me?" The priest shook his head and answered, "No, boy, why are you getting up this time of night? Go back to sleep." It happened again and again. The third time, Eli told him, "If you hear the voice again, it's gotta be God. Just say, 'Lord, Your servant's listening.'"[4]

Likewise, if God speaks to you in the middle of the night, say, "Lord, your servant's listening." Are there areas of denial in your life? Do little dark corners exist in your daily habits? Are thoughts lurking in your mind, sitting there unresolved? They are likely the reason you have problems with your wife or difficulty maintaining friendships, or why you bounce from one job to another, always thinking the ideal situation will crop up at the next place.

Yet the answer lies right in front of you: God's baptism of fire. That's the baptism few people crave, because it means complete change. Fire burns away impurities, the kind you can't help but pick up walking through this world. Jacob got hit with fire the night he received his new name. At first he resisted, which is why he wrestled all night with God before he surrendered.

There may be things inside you that you don't even recognize—thoughts, habits, and ways that God wants to remove from you. *Just give me one night,* He says, *and I can do it in a moment. I can burn this garbage out of you.* I tell the women in my congregation, "If the men put their mind into a VCR and showed it, you would die to see what they think." It's true! Men often struggle with lewd thoughts about other women—or other men. They wrestle mightily, never revealing this to a soul. Yet God knows it's there and wants to deliver them.

Deliverance

The Bible says, "And do not be conformed to this world, but be transformed by the renewing of your mind."[5] God is saying, *Here's a new head, a new controlling point,* but to get it, you have to yield to him, just as Jacob did. After they fought all night, God declared, "That's it. I'm tired of this stuff," and *bam!* He knocked Jacob's hip out of joint. Now, that's power! When that happened, Jacob quit fighting. He recognized he had to acknowledge God and lean totally on him before he could change.

Follow Jacob's example and cry out, "Lord, you've got to bless me. You've shown me who I am, and now you've got to bless me, because I don't like what I see." Those words can't be lip service. They have to come from deep down in your heart.

If you will meet God seriously, He'll change your name. He says His children are more than conquerors.[6] So, armed with His power, start facing the stuff that keeps you defeated and trust him to help you overcome. You don't have to be a prisoner to drugs any longer. You don't have to live with the scars of physical or sexual abuse. God says you were created in his image.[7] So don't accept the condemnation of the naysayers who label you "filth."

> *Armed with God's power, start facing the stuff that keeps you defeated and trust Him to help you overcome.*

Many have labored under depression or hurt for years, struggling to find release. That release is in the Spirit of God. You are what God ordained you to be and who he told you to be.

Jesus asked who men said he was. Simon jumped up and declared, "Thou art the Christ, the Son of the living God."[8] Jesus responded, "Blessed are you, Simon Barjona, because flesh and blood did not reveal this to you, but My Father who is in heaven. And I also say to you that you are Peter, and upon this rock I will build My church; and the gates of Hades shall not overpower it."[9]

Jacob wasn't the only one whose name was changed in the Bible. Peter's name change proved equally significant. *Simon* in Greek means something similar to "flaky," but *Peter* means "rock." As you submit to God's power and receive his revelation of who you are, you'll see that you're no longer flaky, but solid.

God changed me from Eddie Lee Longhead to Bishop Eddie Long, pastor of a thriving Atlanta congregation, no longer afraid to look anyone in the eye. He changed Jacob to Israel, Simon to Peter. And now he's ready to change you.

Say aloud, "I am a man. As Philippians 4:13 says, 'I can do all things through Him who strengthens me.' God says I'm a rock. He says I'm an heir to his kingdom. I'm his son. I have a new name, and I will forever praise God for giving it to me."

Now, go and live up to your name! Pastor Dale Bronner will tell you more about it in the next chapter, and what to do if you start falling back into the "old you."

GET UP AND MOVE ON

by Dale Bronner

I once knew a minister who sinned openly. I didn't learn this through rumors; he told me himself. Worst of all, he expressed no regret over his actions and apparently lacked any intention of changing his lewd behavior. I knew nothing of his circumstances, only the deeds he practically bragged about. It greatly offended me.

"He isn't even worthy to be called a minister," I griped to a close friend one afternoon. "That man is playing with God. Mark my words, he's going to be struck down. The Word says that as sure as the sun rises in the east, God will not be mocked. He'd better watch himself!"

Driving home after that conversation, I felt the Holy Spirit's conviction about my words washing over me. Suddenly a verse of Scripture flashed through my mind: "Who are you to judge the servant of another? To his own master he stands or falls; and stand he will, for the Lord is able to make him stand."[1] This sounded so clearly in my mind that it could have come through a megaphone. I pulled to the side of the road and peered into the backseat to see if someone had hidden there. I repented right then. I realized that I was about to give up on that brother when God was just getting started.

Over the next four years, God caused a tremendous change in that pastor's heart. The Lord brought him out of his error, raised him up, and restored him to righteousness. Today God is proving his love through the mighty ways he uses him. What I saw was a sinner in his temporary fallen state, but the Lord saw him in a restored condition. Thank God for what he sees in us! Thank God He doesn't readily quit on us!

> **God doesn't quit on you. So why would you ever consider quitting on yourself?**

Now apply the moral of that story personally: If God doesn't quit on you, why would you ever consider quitting on yourself? When you sin, God doesn't look at that as the end of your life. He knows you'll make mistakes. He stands ready to help you correct them and move on. Since you are his child, he will discipline you, like a good parent. Painful, yes. But God's goal is to see you restored, revived, rehabilitated, and resurrected!

When you stumble, that's not the time to sit and moan over your lot in life in a giant "pity party." It's time to declare, "I have to get up, because my life isn't over. I can't let myself or my family down or fail my God. I must go on!" God isn't looking only for people who can have faith in him, but also for people in whom he can have faith. He wants to depend on us to do his will.

As long as you're fighting, you're never defeated. The apostle Paul wrote, "I have fought the good fight, I have finished the course, I have kept the faith."[2] If you keep fighting like Paul, you'll never lose. The minute you quit, a winner is declared, and it's the other side. Whether you get knocked down or you fall down, you must get up to finish the race. You must hold on to your faith.

Jesus told Peter that Satan wanted to sift him like wheat, but he finished with these crucial words: "But I have prayed for you, that your faith may not fail; and you, when once you have turned again, strengthen your brothers."[3] The good news is that he's still praying—for you and me. "Who is the one who condemns? Christ Jesus is he who died, yes, rather who was raised, who is at the right hand of God, who also intercedes for us."[4]

When we accept his grace, we can stand and move on in his strength. I don't mean this as an encouragement to sin. But if we do sin, we have a remedy. "My little children, I am writing these things to you that you may not sin. And if anyone sins, we have an Advocate with the Father, Jesus Christ the righteous."[5]

As long as you're fighting you're never defeated.

So, we don't rejoice because we fall, but we can take heart in the promise of restoration. *We don't drown by falling in the water; we drown by staying there.* We don't have to stay in the water. Christ the eternal Life guard stands ready to respond to our pleas for help. The love he embodies "does not rejoice in unrighteousness, but rejoices with the truth; bears all things, believes all things, hopes all things, endures all things. Love never fails."[6]

Even when *we* fail, God's unconditional love for us never fails. Certainly Jesus' disciples weren't perfect. Their members included His betrayer. Another denied him, and by that time the rest had left him. Still Jesus showed them deep compassion and concern. In his prayer in the Garden of Gethsemane, he told his Father, "I pray for them. I am not praying for the world, but for those you have given me, for they are yours. . . . My prayer is not for them alone. I pray also for those who will believe in me through their message."[7]

If you believe in Christ and have confessed him as your Savior, it's because he prayed for you. Despite your mistakes, he is *still* praying for you.

Your Adversary

While there are good influences in life to encourage you, such as the supportive prayers of the body of Christ, the devil also eagerly roams around. His goal is to make you feel like such a failure when you falter that you'll never try to succeed again. His weapons are guilt, shame, and condemnation, which he uses to destroy your confidence and self-esteem and make you feel unworthy.

The idea that you're a total failure is a lie! Everything your spiritual enemy says is a lie. Consider the words of the apostle John: "For God did not send the Son into the world to judge the world, but that the world should be saved through Him."[8] The Lord is not interested in condemning you but in seeing you saved and delivered.

If your life seems dark and dismal, remember that the picture isn't complete. The darkest parts will only serve as a backdrop when the Lord's glory shines through. Patience often comes from trials. Look at this incredible promise: "For from of old they have not heard nor perceived by ear, / Neither has the eye seen a God besides Thee, / Who acts in behalf of the one who waits for Him."[9]

Think of yourself as a seed. Unless you're an expert in horticulture, when you look at a seed, you have no idea what the plant will look like in full bloom. You wouldn't know a turnip seed from a collard seed, or the germ of a red pepper from a green one. But you don't have to be a farmer to know that seeds reproduce their own kind. So all you have to do is plant the seed and wait for God to grow it. Then you'll see its exact form.

Jesus used the seed to illustrate this parable about heaven:

The kingdom of heaven is like a mustard seed, which a man took and sowed in his field; and this is smaller than all other seeds; but when it is full grown, it is larger than the garden plants, and becomes a tree, so that the birds of the air come and nest in its branches.[10]

Does that give you a better appreciation for the enormous potential of a seed? You may start like that tiny grain of mustard. But as God continues his work, he builds you into a mighty tree who becomes a refuge for others. Learn to measure yourself not by where you are or where you've been but by where you're going. God isn't through with you yet. Losers look at what they're going *through*. Winners look at what they're going *to*.

After Job lost everything, he easily could have reached the conclusion that God was finished in his life. Yet he stands out as a man of patience and endurance. His words still carry hope for all believers: "But He knows the way I take; / When He has tried me, I shall come forth as gold."[11] Even when Job's circumstances pointed downward, his outlook aimed upward. Instead of looking at life as dark and hopeless, he saw gold. But gold will not jump into your hands. You have to get down in the dirt and dig for it. Gold is in your future.

Despite his setbacks, Job knew God would work everything for good in his life.[12] You can know the Lord isn't through with you, because you are not through with God. Job remained faithful, knowing he had not finished his life's course. After saying he would come forth as gold, Job continued, "My foot has held fast to His path; / I have kept His way and not turned aside. / I have not departed from the command of His lips; / I have treasured the words of His mouth more than my necessary food."[13] Do you see the significance of Job's words? God will not release you when you refuse to release God. It is God's nature to reward faithfulness.

If you've failed in any area of life, don't despair. You weren't the first to fall, nor will you be the last. All you need is a fresh start. That's what repentance does for us—it gives us a new beginning with God. Confessing our sins and seeking his forgiveness ensure that they are as much a part of ancient history as yesterday.

No matter how hard or how low you've fallen, you can get up and move on. Moses killed an Egyptian, but cold-blooded murder only marked the beginning of God's new work in his life. Abraham slept with his maid Hagar to produce a son, but adultery and presumption didn't stop the Lord from later bringing forth the promised child, Isaac. Samson told a woman his secret and broke covenant with God, but through Samson's death the Almighty brought great judgment on the Philistines. After David sinned with Bathsheba, he thought his

Temporary faults do not define you.

life was over, but the Lord corrected and restored him.

The list of fallen and revived biblical heroes goes on and on. The important point for you to grasp is, if you've fallen so badly you can't get up, at least look up and call on God. He will hear your cry and restore you. "For the Son of Man has come to seek and to save that which was lost."[14] Remember, someone very special is looking for you!

Does Strength or Weakness Define You?

Do you consider yourself weak? When you look in the mirror of self-evaluation, what do you see? Nothing but weaknesses? Forget them for a minute while you write down a list of your strengths. Can't think of any? It may be because you're concentrating too much on your weaknesses. Everyone has them. However, like the pastor I mentioned in the beginning of this chapter, you need to understand this: *Temporary faults do not define you!*

Despite your weaknesses, you possess strength. Despite your present, you're reaching for a golden future.

In our athletically driven society, people chase after the god of "number one," as if a single victory can eliminate all their other weaknesses. *Balance is the key to life.* If everyone were academically inclined, who would do the maintenance on our cars and trucks? If everyone were mechanically inclined, who would write our books, sing our songs, and teach our children?

> *The power of the weak comes in the declaration of strength.*

Everyone has strengths. Even if you consider yourself weak, you have strengths elsewhere that you just haven't discovered yet. Scripture shows that strength comes from not identifying with weakness. When it was time to go to war, the prophet Joel declared, "Let the weakling say, 'I am strong!'"[15] The power of the weak comes in the declaration of strength.

Get It Together

Look at what this book has been teaching you. How do you view yourself? If a particular name could sum up your life, what would it be? Would you choose a great one? Think of Abraham, whose name is associated with "faith." Or Elijah, "prophecy." Solomon is synonymous with "wisdom." Moses reminds us of "law." Ezekiel left an impression of "visionary." John's life left behind the character of "love."

You can grumble and complain that you'll never amount to anything, but I guarantee that if you pursue a name that denotes strength, people will remember you for your strength! So stop calling yourself dumb, stupid, lazy, no-good fatso, loafer, or worthless playboy. It's no joking matter. You will produce behavior consistent with your name.

A change in name represents a change in status or nature. Soldiers advance from buck private to private first class to corporal to sergeant to lieutenant. It is important to carry a name that will give you self-respect and purpose. If you are not confident of your identity, others will try to impose a name on you. People can commit sin against you and leave their name on you.

The only way to change your behavior is to change the way you view yourself. Give yourself a new name, and your new name will give you a new identity. Born-again Christians have received the "spirit of adoption."[16] In the kingdom of God, we get a new name, a new family, and a new nature.

That means if you were known as "weak," now you are "strong." Instead of "sinner," you are "the righteousness of Christ." Get rid of any old names that are dragging you down.

Then, identify with Jesus Christ. Take everything that holds you back, every attitude and belief, to the cross. When you lay them down, come away as the new creation you were intended to become.

And keep moving on. Temporary failures are only short-term. Learn from them. Make yesterday's failure the fertilizer for tomorrow's success. There's much more in store for you than what you presently see.

Affirm who God says you are, get up, and move on with him! The cross is the place of exchange, where you trade the old you for the new, where you exchange your sinfulness for Christ's righteousness. Pastor Joel Brooks writes more about this subject in the next chapter.

9

MANHOOD AND CHRISTLIKENESS ARE SYNONYMOUS

by Joel Brooks

Before coming to Christ, our behavior is shaped by hurt, lies, prejudice, rejection, and negative thoughts. Unexpected and unfair things strike people every day. Violence, abuse, and degradation of all kinds plague our society. But while we cannot control such events, we can decide how they will affect us. The central message of this entire book is that, for us, manhood and Christlikeness are synonymous.[1] God's process of making us like Christ is also his process of making each of us a man. The value of Christianity is not what God *gives* us—like health and wealth—but what he *makes* us. As Christians, we each have the authority to become a son of God, a real man.

God's process for making us men is the cross. We have to figuratively go to the cross in prayer, unburden ourselves of everything holding us to this earth and to past experiences, and trust God that we'll come away with a different perspective, attitude, and way of life. And we do this even *after* we are saved, as we continue to shed the old ways and walk in the new. There is a fleshly part of us that conflicts with God and perceives him as an adversary and hindrance to our happiness. The cross is the cure for our flesh, our selfishness.

▲ ▲ ▲ ▲ ▲

The value of Christianity is not what God gives us—like health and wealth—but what He makes us.

▼ ▼ ▼ ▼ ▼

The cross is part of a tree. Adam and Eve lost their good standing with God at a tree when what seemed good actually meant destruction. Jesus won back our right standing with God on the tree, which looked like defeat but proved to be victory. Although we may try to avoid it, the cross is not the symbol of death and failure it appears to be. Instead of death, Jesus gives us life. Instead of helplessness, the cross gives us power.

The cross is always optional. Some people talk about the "cross they have to bear," but hardships are not a cross, nor is sickness, disease, or poverty. Jesus took those things in our place when he hung on the cross. He said to take up your cross daily, which means to go to him of your own free will, depend on him, trust in him, and die to yourself—to your imaginations, fantasies, and secret sins. It's not something that is forced on you involuntarily. It is your choice to decide what to do when you face a crossroads, a cross. The cross symbolizes the choice to die to self and live on a new higher level of the Christlike life.

The cross means surrender. That means you follow the leader, Christ, no matter how tough the circumstances. In other words, no griping! The untrained soul always murmurs, complains, and accuses when he is unsatisfied, unhappy, or uncomfortable. He cannot endure because he lacks hope. He cannot see, so he cannot believe. He ends up blaming others. The unsaved person blames God. The saved person whose mind and character have not been renewed in the Word tends to blame the leadership.

Taking up the Cross

Since I have gone to the cross, even as a pastor years after my salvation, God has worked tremendously in my life. I discovered that not everyone was willing to go with me and that to lay my life down meant I'd be losing some friendships.

Jesus said, "Do not think that I came to bring peace on the

> _Your cross is to follow Jesus first, at the possible expense of every other relationship in your life._

earth; I did not come to bring peace, but a sword. For I came to set a man against his father, and a daughter against her mother, and a daughter-in-law against her mother-in-law; and a man's enemies will be the members of his household."[2]

This doesn't mean that you are to be at war with your family. But your cross is to follow Jesus first, at the possible expense of every other relationship in your life. The gospel affects your outlook and philosophy of life. Every conviction you hold becomes based on the Word, not on social dictates or theories. That means people from the old crowd probably aren't going to like you much anymore.

God's touch sometimes changes your world. Other times it changes you and moves you out of your world. That means rejection from others can be your birth into a new phase of life. When a woman's womb rejects her baby at nine months because the fetus has outgrown it, we don't call it rejection. We rejoice over new birth.

Life's seasons often start with the labor pains of rejection and discomfort. It may not seem like it, but it is the moment we have long awaited. Today's harsh circumstances may be the womb of tomorrow. And just as with the baby who struggles into a new world, some of the "old you" may be left behind. So will some of your old friends. People don't change in groups, and your change may cost you the group's approval.

> *God's touch sometimes changes your world. Other times it changes you and moves you out of your world.*

No matter what the opposition, you cannot compromise the gospel, because that would sacrifice the worthiness of the cross. The gospel teaches we must love all people regardless of race or color. To try to cater to people instead of Christ keeps you away from the cross. Things nailed to the cross cannot make it to the other side. Your "hang-ups" must be hung up so that you can be a free man.

Many teachers who have brought tremendous blessings to me are white. Had I held on to past prejudices, I would have rejected part of Jesus' provision for me. Isaiah said that our teachers would be in front of our eyes, but we would also hear a voice behind us, saying, "This is the way, walk in it."[3] So when I listen to teachers, I look solely for the Holy Spirit's anointing that makes Jesus and the things of God more real. Color is no longer the issue it once was, since going to the cross.

The Only Pattern

Every believer is to be formed in the image of Jesus. He is the Master. His pattern of victory and promotion is the blueprint for everyone who desires to be a real man. First the Cross, then the Resurrection.

The cross is difficult for unrenewed minds because of its sensation of loss. Many men make the mistake of thinking that if they choose to take up their cross and follow Christ, they are losing out, giving in, or becoming a wimp.

That is a lie. People have attacked Christianity for centuries as a "religion for wimps." They claim our lives symbolize defeat, finishing last, living on bare necessities, accepting abuse, never trying to better our circumstances, and mildly accepting anything that comes our way. How ironic that someone who has never walked in our shoes claims to know so much about our lives!

Some even blame the Christian faith for slavery and the present condition of African-Americans in the world.

But Christianity is not to blame. Lifeless, defeated "churchianity" is the culprit. Religious people perpetrated slavery, but true Christians rose up and abolished it. We all know the civil rights movement sprang up in the church. The Bible overflows with terms like victory, overcoming, triumph, fighting, wrestling, warfare, and armor. What many have mistakenly labeled as loss and defeat is really victory and gain.

It takes a man to stand and proclaim his Christianity in the midst of this selfish, materialistic, pagan world. Only a man can stand when others challenge his position in Christ. Only a man can work to put away historical divisions between black and white, man and woman, Jew and Gentile. Only a man can persevere through personal difficulties, self-doubts, and the devil's attacks.

And for the man who endures pressure and opposition, there are great rewards. Standing for the right thing for God on earth causes you to be chosen by God in heaven. People talk a lot about calling and purpose, but they need to remember that the Bible says "many are *called,* but few are *chosen.*"[4] It also says that God called things that are not as they were. So when God calls you, that means you have not yet become what he called you to be. You must become involved with his conversion process so he can resurrect you into the *called* man that he has *chosen.*

That means facing a crossroads, leaving your agenda, emotions, and prejudices at the cross, and coming out the other side as the Christlike man God intended you to be.

There are bound to be times when you still feel like less than a man, when you let others down or you let yourself down. In the next section you are going to learn about getting ahead in life, and getting on with your new manhood. Just remember, going to the cross in total surrender, doing what appears to be weak, is the way to become a strong man who can withstand the toughest opposition.

Part Four

GETTING AHEAD

The same Lord is Lord of all and bestows his riches upon all who call upon him.

Romans 10:12 RSV

10

I HAVE OVERCOME

by Clinton Utterbach

We shall overcome.
We shall overcome
We shall overcome some day.

That beautiful song is haunting, causing pride to swell in the heart of every black American. The great anthem of the civil rights movement still stirs us like no other. I respect, admire, and am grateful to the men and women who laid down their lives to start bringing down the grossly unjust social system that suppressed the black community in this country. But with respect toward everyone who fought and struggled for freedom, I must say that it's because of Jesus Christ that today I can truthfully sing, "I have overcome."

I'm a long way from slavery, sharecropping, and Selma, and thousands of blacks are with me. We're doing more than eating at lunch counters, drinking from public fountains, and sitting in the front of buses. We're overcoming circumstances every day by the power of God.

The true church of our Lord Jesus Christ is multiracial, multiethnic, and multicultural. In the apostle Paul's day, this vibrant, powerful body turned the world upside down. They were true overcomers, even though they were in the minority. Their power grew despite fierce oppression and widespread martyrdom. Two centuries after the death of the apostle John, the emperor Constantine declared Christianity the official religion of Rome—the nation that was once its leading oppressor!

▲ ▲ ▲ ▲ ▲

To overcome the difficulties facing us today, we're all, regardless of our color or culture, going to have to change from within and seek God's solutions and overcoming power.

▼ ▼ ▼ ▼ ▼

That's the kind of strong faith with which I identify. Its principles freed me from the grip of sin and racism and helped me understand that I am a spirit being; I have a soul, and I live in a body. As God's child, I'm his offspring, created by the same Spirit who breathed life into Adam. Once I grasped this truth, the color of my skin no longer mattered, nor what anyone else said about it. I had discovered my identity.

Still, Christianity faces a dilemma. After so many years of subjugation, discrimination, and frustration, the black race in America is looking for the road to emancipation. The black male, in particular, seeks his manhood—the state of being male, adult, self-reliant, and courageous.

Many strident voices in the African-American community promote separation and self-reliance. Social programs have failed to end black-on-black crime, drug abuse, illegitimate pregnancies, and illiteracy. Society's racial climate, the degeneration of the family, and self-destructive behaviors cry out for immediate solutions. But we cannot ignore the lesson of history: The end does not justify the means. To overcome the difficulties facing us today, we're all, regardless of our color or culture, going to have to change from *within* and seek God's solutions and overcoming power.

Hostility Is No Solution

I was born in Harlem Hospital and raised in the South Bronx, in the area now known as Fort Apache. Growing up in a multicultural school, I never thought much about race until I reached dating age. Then the difference between the races struck home. Yet dating relationships were the least of my problems.

Even though I was an honor student in junior high school, my Caucasian adviser deliberately recommended a school of lesser reputation than the one I should have attended. Later, two Jewish teachers recognized my ability and tried to convince me to transfer to a better academic environment. I ignored their advice. My lack of initiative prevented me from pursuing higher education, which limited my upward mobility.

By the 1960s, like most of my brothers, I lived for "the cause." The civil rights era was a time of great expectations but also of great naïveté on my part. I thought that merely exposing the plight of black people would bring sympathy from most Americans. I believed that everyone would understand our situation and correct the problem.

Then I watched the killing of my heroes, like John and Bobby Kennedy, who had advanced our cause, and our great advocate, Martin Luther King Jr. I realized that those in charge of the "system" weren't playing games. They weren't about to change willingly. That realization embittered me. Had I not grown up in a Christian home, I likely would have resorted to the tactics of radicals who blew up buildings to vent their rage.

I didn't act on my angry impulses, but for many, the wounds of that era still fester. That's why increasing numbers of African-Americans are now turning to the Black Muslims. I understand those who feel persecuted, discriminated against, and hopeless about achievement in a "white-run" society. I can see the attraction of a group that provides rehabilitation and counseling to prisoners, drug addicts, and street gangs. On the surface, it appears good that Black Muslims bring surveillance and protection to certain drug-controlled neighborhoods and a sense of acceptance to a people long denied it.

Yet those are hollow accomplishments, because all the good works in the world won't save one soul from hell. Only Christ can do that. He saved me and taught me the real way to overcome.

The Muslim leadership's harsh criticism and racial invective against all whites damage their credibility and hurt society. No person can truthfully say that we don't need a brother or sister of another race or culture. The globe is too small for separatism. John 3:16 is true, that God so loved the *world* that he gave his Son to die on the cross, and that means he died for *everybody*.

Black Muslims' criticism of Jewish people is particularly regrettable. Leaders of the Nation of Islam suggest that Jews exert ironclad control over black entertainers, professionals, and intellectuals, and that they are the hands holding us back. They suggest that blacks need to sever those hands to be free.

It's easy to understand the harsh reaction of the Jewish community to this hate-filled message. The truth is that when nobody else would rent to us, sell to us, or represent us in court, the Jews interacted with us. And they still do. Good Jewish men and women, like those who helped guide me, greatly aided the powerful civil rights legislation of the 1960s. Instead of our opposition, we owe them a debt of gratitude.

Where Can We Turn?

Many black leaders who once criticized this nation for its inability to cure poverty and improve education in our communities now realize our country grapples with other problems as well, such as the economy, the environment, and a host of troublesome foreign conflicts. We cannot rely on the government alone to respond adequately to the ongoing needs of a particular segment of our population. We can't just count on government.

Nor can we overlook that rugged individualism and determined initiative that made America great in the first place. Self-reliance is, indeed, a virtue. All the races who came to these shores had to work hard and compete to become part of this society's productive fabric. When others can't or won't help, it's always proper to dig in your heels and help yourself. But while self-help is a goal, it's not the complete answer, either. We can't just count on self-reliance.

Christ teaches us complete dependence—not on man, but on God. The Lord's willingness and ability to get involved in men's affairs is a concept we can grasp only by faith (and the Lord even has to give us the faith). This faith must be strong enough to believe that God will deliver us from our oppressors. Males rush to fight their enemies, but men of faith wait for the Almighty's answer.

The mob that crucified Christ made a terrible mistake. Among other things, they fumed over his lack of vigorous opposition. Instead they cried, "Give us Barabbas!" Barabbas was a man jailed for violent opposition to Rome. Today, many young males and others in the black community reject Christianity for essentially the same reason—the church's lack of vigorous, militant opposition to today's perceived oppressors. Yet Rome became Christian through men overcoming with *God's* power, not *human* strength.

There can be no argument that we live in a Euro-American–dominated culture, where many blacks and other minorities have not had the power and wealth to sustain an acceptable existence. Nor has it helped that the organized Christian church, which should have offered direction to young black men, has been full of racism, intolerance, and hypocrisy. We can't just count on an institutionalized church.

God's true, holy church is made up of individuals who have a spiritual relationship with Him through the person of Jesus Christ. It's this *true* church that will usher in His kingdom on earth.

The church that existed during the first century after Christ's birth was such a group. As people, they had their problems. But as true Christians, they arrived at some good solutions.

A conflict arose between the Hebrews and Greeks regarding the distribution of goods among the believers in that early church. The solution is noteworthy. The apostles didn't select representatives of each culture to negotiate a deal. Nor did each nationality launch a campaign of cultural superiority. No, they selected men full of faith and the Holy Spirit, who ministered with godly wisdom.[1] That's the same kind of men we need today. We can count on God, and we can count on Him to work in society through godly men.

It Starts on the Inside of You

Martin Luther King Jr.'s vision is still desirable: that of peaceful coexistence of all groups in our society. We must never forget that there are remedies to racism, teenage pregnancy, welfare, drugs, crime, and black rage. The true, lasting social remedies are those that stem from a personal relationship with Jesus Christ, not militant opposition to social oppression.

Courage sometimes manifests itself as fearlessness in the face of danger or heroism on the battlefield. But on other occasions, brave people demonstrate their courage by their ability to forgive, even when forgiveness is unpopular. Appreciating the value of others with whom you may disagree can prove more powerful than the greatest demonstration of opposition.

> *We can count on God, and we can count on Him to work in society through godly men.*

My manhood is not defined by society's expectations, other people, or the American culture. It comes from God's standards, as outlined in His Word and exemplified by the life of Jesus. When Christ had the power to command legions of angels to set him free, but instead chose to sacrifice himself on the cross, he established a higher law that has its roots in God's powerful, mysterious love.

The true, lasting social remedies are those that stem from a personal relationship with Jesus Christ, not militant opposition to social oppression.

That love is still at work, sparking a revival among America's ethnic minorities and enabling us as individuals to overcome. This has been going on for many years among many congregations across the nation. The common element is true trust in God.

The true church will one day operate in a brand-new, unified fashion by which God conquers old barriers of race and culture. This change from a fleshly, divided nature into a unified, spiritual body will come from an old source—individual trust in God. The men I identify with today have great trust in God and tremendous courage. These are the kind of men who, in the apostle Paul's day, turned the world upside down. I'm ready. Are you?

Joseph Ripley has more to say about overcoming circumstances to achieve excellence in life in the next chapter. He is one of those men who is leading others to rise above society's pitfalls and raise the standard of their lives.

11

RAISE THE STANDARD!

by Joseph Ripley

I used to play music for a living, cookin' and cruisin' my way through the nightclubs and thinking I had grabbed the gusto in life—when in reality that world had me in its clutches. When God found me, my name topped the "Ten Most Wanted" list of America's credit bureaus. I thirsted for the world's ways, but all I had to show for my worldly lifestyle were empty pockets and a pile of bills that seemed to reach to the moon.

Swallowing my pride, I turned my back on the music world and went to work at McDonald's. People can laugh about "flipping burgers," but I learned that any kind of honest work is honorable. It pays your bills, feeds your family, and, most important, builds character. That was where I started to learn how to move up in life for real, instead of just pretending.

The Bible warns us not to despise the day of small beginnings.[1] Some men may have jobs that look small: convenience store clerk, custodian, or boiler room worker. But God can use you no matter what your occupation.

And if you don't want to be stuck at the bottom, you can rise to the top through desire, ambition, and God's direction. You can realize and enjoy all the benefits the Lord wants you to have. God is rich to all who call upon him.[2]

God is a champion. And he wants to be your partner if you'll let him. The God I serve isn't some unreachable, untouchable force who floats around like Casper the ghost. Let him fill you with his Holy Spirit, change your attitude into one of respect for your superiors, put a smile on your face, and make you diligent in your work. Before you know it, you'll rise to heights you never thought possible. Through His Word, God will meet all your needs. He already desires that. He says to you, "Beloved, I pray that in all respects you may prosper and be in good health, just as your soul prospers."[3]

Whatever it is you do, do it to the best of your ability. Then strive to exceed that standard. Carry yourself with dignity, decency, and respect for others, despite how anyone else acts. You don't have to follow the crowd. No matter where you go, you'll find lazy slobs who don't respect anyone else, their achievements, or their hard work. Those cynics gripe about how hard they have it, how underpaid they are, and how everyone else gets all the breaks. Don't fall into their trap!

You can rise to the top through desire, ambition, and God's direction.

The Bible teaches us to have respect for those in authority. You must speak to them with honor and hold them in high esteem because of their position. Even if you don't like the president of the company, respect his office. Call him "Mr. President." It won't hurt you, and it may help you. "The king's heart is in the hand of the Lord."[4] I believe that verse applies to all who are in seats of authority. And if you have grace in God's eyes, he can give you grace in other people's eyes.

You may have been at your job for months, even years, working faithfully, always on time, obedient to your supervisors, helpful to your coworkers, and showing the joy of the Lord by the way you conduct yourself. Bam! God can move on the president to call for your file: "How long has that brother been with us? Bring me his file. Let's see . . . perfect attendance, never late, no calling in with excuses, superior job review, good attitude. How come I never noticed this man before?"

Well, he won't wrestle with that last question very long. He knows you're there now. He will wonder: If you have this great of an attitude pushing a broom, what will happen if you're upstairs, pushing a pencil, or pushing a few buttons on the keyboards that operate the machinery? If you don't think God can do that, it's only because you've never tried his ways.

We need righteous men to go from the boiler room to the boardroom. If God's

▲   ▲   ▲   ▲   ▲

Whatever it is you do, do it to the best of your ability.

▼   ▼   ▼   ▼   ▼

men were in charge, you wouldn't check into hotels and find X-rated garbage on the TV because of money-hungry owners. You wouldn't find condoms in the schoolhouse because of administrators who lack moral values. Nor would you find drugs flowing through the streets because corrupt officials take bribes to look the other way. The Word says, "By the blessing of the upright a city is exalted, But by the mouth of the wicked it is torn down."[5] We need *our* men in charge!

Not only will God exalt you in your job, but he will also protect you. When I had worked my way up to assistant manager at McDonald's, I requested a shift change so I could take care of some personal chores. That made the manager mad. He didn't tell me directly, but the other assistant manager warned, "Joe, you'd better watch out. He's got it in for you. He's going to try to get you fired." I thanked him for letting me know, but I didn't have any hard feelings toward the manager.

Still, one night I was filling out my cash report at the end of the night shift, and the words and images of the prophet Daniel came to me. I felt as if I were back in Babylon, watching a hand writing on the wall, and I knew the manager's days in his job were numbered. Less than two weeks later, when I went to work, the area supervisor was there. I greeted him and asked, "Where's the manager?"

He shook his head and said, "We just fired him a couple of hours ago. You're going to be running things here for a while."

You see what I mean? The Word says, "'No weapon that is formed against you shall prosper; / And every tongue that accuses you in judgment you will condemn. / This is the heritage of the servants of the LORD, / And their vindication is from Me,' declares the LORD."[6] The Bible doesn't promise that no weapons will be formed against you. But it guarantees the ones formed won't prosper in the long run.

That doesn't necessarily mean you'll always have a job or always get exactly the job you want. But it does mean that if you belong to God, he is committed to meeting your needs, and he is willing to give you great favor in the eyes of your supervisors.

A Decision Away

When the Lord saved me, I wasn't famous. I didn't have a radio program. I didn't pastor a large, growing church. I was so dumb that all I knew how to do was obey God.

People often like to complicate theology, making it something so difficult that only the privileged few can grasp it. While it takes time to mature as a Christian and develop a faithful walk with God, keep this in mind: the goal is to make God's life part of yours.

Men approach me constantly, wanting to know how to be successful in business, as husbands and fathers, or just as men in general. I could talk about the need for professionalism in every area of your existence or about how everyone needs to walk in the Spirit. But if I had to boil it down to one factor, you may be surprised to learn you're not ten years or 10,000 miles away from it. You're just one little decision away.

That decision is simple. It's right in this statement. Say it aloud as you read: "God, I'm going all the way with You. I commit to You. My heart's desire as a [businessman, plumber, bricklayer, carpenter, attorney, etc.] is to glorify You through the skills and gifts You've given me. I submit them to You, Lord, and ask You to anoint them, enhance them, and develop them. I commit my plans to You and acknowledge You in all my ways. Your Word says You will direct my path. Thank you, Lord."

Imagine being a businessman and letting the Lord direct your path. There are no limits to what God can do as you obey Him. "Eye has not seen and ear has not heard, and which have not entered the heart of man, all that God has prepared for those who love Him."[7] The Lord wants you to get accustomed to allowing him to direct your life in whatever few things you may have. Show him you're willing to listen now, and he'll stick with you as a partner when you step into the big leagues.

This applies to many more things than money. The most important things in our society have nothing to do with money. But the answers come from the same Source: "The one who is in you is greater than the one who is in the world."[8]

It's one thing to quote that verse, but believing it is a different matter. Many of my black brothers believe there's a concerted, sinister, and systematic effort to oppress and hold them back. But from God's perspective, such plots don't matter, even when they're real. Do you believe God's plan is to give us a future and a hope?[9] Do you believe you have something greater than others?[10] So if some man is trying to hold us back, *so what?*

I'm not trying to deny that racism exists. It works from every corner and angle of society. But blacks aren't its only victims. I've traveled to southern California, Texas, Louisiana, and states on the Canadian border where Hispanics, Native Americans, Jews, and others suffer its sting too. Various social agencies, action groups, and urban leagues have identified the problem, but few know of any solution. It goes back to a principle of God's kingdom that Jesus told Nicodemus: "What is born of the flesh is flesh, and what is born of the spirit is spirit."[11]

Social action won't change anyone's heart. If men are full of hatred, spite, maliciousness, and racism, you can't legislate it out of them. The Congress can declare discrimination illegal by a 535-0 vote, the president can sign an executive order, and the Supreme Court can back them up—and it won't change one man's heart.

The main reason we see urban decay is that we live as victims instead of men in charge.

I have nothing against government. Government is God's plan to maintain order in society. But we have to stop looking to the government to solve our problems and take our signals from the Almighty. As a community leader, I know about the problems of modern society. Our school systems are crying, county agencies are whining, and municipalities are sagging under the weight of the challenge. But I believe the main reason we see urban decay is that we have bought the devil's lie and live as victims instead of men in charge.

I remember when I first moved into an area ten minutes from the Atlanta airport. It was the American dream come to life. Residential communities sprang up everywhere, and many of them were racially mixed. But then "transition" came, white flight occurred, and African-Americans inundated the area.

Why is it that when the predominant racial makeup changes, an area suddenly is "in decline"? Why do the property values have to decrease? Why don't we know how to maintain landscapes better than anyone else? How come we can't go out and knock a shingle or two in place on our roofs? Why can't we keep the windows clean? Why don't we patronize our businesses? Why don't we start them? Why don't we seek excellence?

All the potential to bring renaissance to our cities exists within those areas if the people will only believe God.

I've driven through the suburbs on the weekend. I see shopping malls with traffic jams of humanity. The places with the big-screen TVs showing major sporting events have packed parking lots. The little outdoor cafes are so jammed that people are milling around on the sidewalk, waiting for a seat. From my experience in the restaurant business, I look at those places and know the owners are turning over thousands of dollars in an hour. So, my African-American brother, why can't you own one of those businesses? There's no law against it!

All the potential to bring renaissance to our cities exists within those areas if the people will only believe God. We can turn back the damnable lie of the devil that says that because black folks are in an area, the property values decline and all business investment should stay away. That is why God wants you full of his Word. If those outside investors don't want to come in, why don't *you* be an investor? You may find it hard to believe you can do it. But as long as you sit and think, instead of taking action, I guarantee it will never happen.

Faithfulness

The ability, power, and fortitude to bring positive change in your life start with a single scriptural principle: "He who is faithful in a very little thing is faithful also in much."[12] Careful with your dimes and quarters? You'll be the same with thousands of dollars. Spending those extra fifteen minutes in the Word instead of channel surfing on the TV? You'll soon reap the rewards as God shows you bigger things about Himself.

Faithfulness comes from commitment. Our society cries out for men who are committed to their jobs; to standards of good manhood; to ethical, businesslike conduct; to God. When you make commitments—say them aloud, pledge to live by them, and follow through with them—you'll raise your personal standards.

I can look around any city in America and see how few men are willing to raise their personal standards, even though it's not that difficult. Stop carrying yourself around like a slovenly bum. Get a shave and a haircut. Learn to have the right kind of pride in the way you carry and present yourself. Stop bellyaching about your bad home, your lack of education, or your poor prospects.

If you lack education, apply yourself to learning. Read a book for fifteen or twenty minutes a day. Stop making those worthless excuses about never having time. If I followed you around twenty-four hours a day, I'll bet I could find you wasting three or four of them. Ever heard about the foreign-language training programs that can have you speaking common phrases in Spanish, German, French, Italian, or Japanese in just fifteen or twenty minutes a day? Just listen to a cassette tape, a little at a time, and over time you can master the language. While you're at it, check out the colleges and adult education programs in your area and have the humility to go back to school, if that's what will move you toward your goals.

How do you think long-term investors accumulate huge nest eggs? They take a little portion and put it aside in stocks or bonds, mutual funds, or other investments. Then they commit to add to it gradually while putting all the dividends back into their fund. Ten, fifteen, and twenty years go by, and suddenly their investment adds up. It's not because they're so brilliant; they simply act with faithfulness and commitment.

I'm talking about money because I know your pocketbook gets your attention. But we need men who will transfer their faithfulness in money and professional performance to things that matter, men who will stand up for God and proclaim the truth, men who will teach their children the Bible and be the spiritual heads of their households, men who will be courageous in their witness for Christ.

America's homes especially need men who will prove their faithfulness to marriage and family. You need to learn how to treasure your wife. The Bible warns us not to deal treacherously with the wife of our youth.[13] After all, you paid the price. Before she was your wife, you were willing to kill for her! Don't tell me the thrill is gone. You spent your life looking for it, and now you've got it, so get with it!

Too many men treat their wives like a piece of merchandise from a discount store. They take something of value and mark it down. They devalue their wives, turning something precious beyond belief into a dumping ground for their egos. The feminist movement may be off base, but the reason it got off the ground to begin with is that men didn't live up to their responsibilities.

You must come to realize the potential and power that exist when a husband and wife are together in agreement to follow God. Treasure your wife, nourish her, and protect her. Don't go out and dress yourself up like a crown prince and leave her looking like Aunt Jemima on the farm.

You need to spend quality time with your children too. Why do you think so many angry kids cruise the streets, shooting, stealing, and carjacking? No matter what their age, children need someone to spend time with them. Television, books, and magazines can never impart what you can as their father. Talk to your children. Pick them up, hug them, praise them, encourage them, and let them know how much they mean to you. Most of all, let them know how important God is to you.

The world is dying to see Christ alive in his children. But they'll never respect the church as they should until they see Christians faithfully walking in the name of the Lord Jesus—not ashamed of the gospel of Christ but willing to stand boldly for his name.

Does that sound like a pipe dream to you in the chaos of the 1990s? It's not. I'm already seeing it occur. The Christian men's movement that is sweeping the nation is prime evidence of God at work. Our church started its weekly men's meeting nearly ten years ago, and we've seen remarkable results.

Similar things are happening in other churches across the nation. Great miracles are unfolding that don't make newspaper headlines or get on the evening news. But God is moving, bringing revival to America, and all because men have started to make the right choice to follow Him.

Once I was pretending I was cool, a man's man, but today I take more pride in what God has done *inside* me, in my marriage, in my kids, and how he has led me in my career. It all began with the decision I made. You can make the same decision and not settle for being cool only on the outside—but on the inside as well.

Change your belief about yourself, change your actions in relation to the world around you, and you will become one of the new breed of men who are collectively changing our entire culture. Also, look in the next chapter at what Dwight Pate did—starting out as a homeless man and rising in every area of his manhood. If we can do it you can do it!

Part Five

THE CHANGING CULTURE

He who takes refuge in Me shall inherit the land.

Isaiah 57:13

BLACK MEN, RISE UP!

by Dwight D. Pate

I wrote the following words as a frustrated teenager sitting under a pecan tree on a Louisiana plantation:

A New Day

I hold my head in the air;
it used to be toward the ground.
I walk straight through the crowd;
I used to walk around.
I can climb mountains.
I can reach my goal; I can think.
I don't have to be told.
I can reach out and express myself.
If you give it to me,
I don't have to accept.
I am a man—a body, a soul.

A child of the 1960s, I grew up amid the century-old remains of the South. As a child and young teenager, I did not have the opportunity to travel far from the plantation town of Tunica—a town so small you cannot find it on a map.

> **For black communities to reach their fullest potential in God's purposes, they must rise on the shoulders of men who not only understand that God has placed them in this nation and at this time in history, but who also embrace their destiny.**

Yet as I learned to read and began watching movies and television, I dreamed of a world outside the plantation system, one where I could walk shoulder to shoulder with men of all races and colors. So, that stifling summer day, God encouraged me with the words of that poem.

Instead of rural areas, many African-Americans grew up in cities with the prejudices and cruelties of the original system that distorted the black man's self-image. But every black man must grasp the truth that his value or worth is not inside him, not in his material possessions, and not inside anyone else's head.

Black men in America need to believe the gospel of Jesus Christ—that they were created to be born again and to show forth God's glory. To be "born again" means to be "born from above." One biblical translation says a born-again man is a "new creature."[1] In modern language, we could say that being born from above is the birth of a new race. Being born again is far beyond being black, white, yellow, or red.

Black Men, Lead Us to Triumph

For black communities to reach their fullest potential in God's purposes, they must rise on the shoulders of men who not only understand that God has placed them in this nation and at this time in history, but who also embrace their destiny. Such men will lead us out of despair and into triumph.

A relevant example of overcoming the enduring sting of slavery can be found in the story of King David. When David and his men returned from a raid to their hometown of Ziklag, they found it burned. Their families had vanished. Their image of community suddenly lay in rubble. As they looked around in dismay, they felt grief and anger. The men were so angry with David, their scapegoat, that they wanted to stone him.[2]

Isn't that similar to what's going on with many black men today? We blame other men for our misfortunes and lack of personal success, all the while forgetting the God who empowers us to triumph over destruction.

The men in David's time (and those in our own) didn't understand that in rebuilding, God always uses one man. Not one building, one woman, or one child—one man! For Ziklag to be rebuilt family by family, God had to have a man for each household. Sadly, most of the men were too busy weeping and griping to rise to the occasion. But the Bible says, "David strengthened himself in the LORD his God."[3]

David became the man of the hour. Consider this amazing feat. In the natural, David had lost everything. Because he was on the run from a jealous king, he didn't have a homeland. He had lost his closest family ties. Now he had lost his wife and children. In other words, he had lost his past, present, and future.

Yet he had something inside that no one could take: he knew how to encourage himself in the Lord while others around him wept, fainted, and wanted to die. What was this internal force? It came from one episode in his past. "Then Samuel took the horn of oil and anointed him in the midst of his brothers; and the Spirit of the LORD came mightily upon David from that day forward."[4] When Samuel anointed David, the anointing that came on his life symbolized the born-again experience that we have in New Testament days. God's Spirit declared David's kingship.

▲ ▲ ▲ ▲ ▲

In the heart of every Christian black man is the spirit of a king.

▼ ▼ ▼ ▼ ▼

The Bible teaches that in the word of a king there is power and also that God has made us kings and priests unto him. That brings us to this riveting truth: *In the heart of every Christian black man is the spirit of a king.*

When I was a homeless man, living in a shack on a parking lot, I wasn't living like a king. But when I was born again, the spirit of a king rose up in me.

Like David, when we receive Christ as our Savior, we receive the anointing of the Holy Spirit. With that anointing, we start being transformed by the renewing of our minds.[5] Yes, we have control over our bodies. Yes, we have control over the stressful situations in which we find ourselves. We're new people with renewed thoughts, feelings, and purposes. These three principles govern our lives as Christians.

New Thoughts. When we are born again by the Spirit of almighty God, he deposits new thoughts in our minds. We don't think as we used to, because his presence makes us different. The Word says, "Have this attitude in yourselves which was also in Christ Jesus."[6]

New Feelings. Through our new birth, God deposits his divine nature in us. The selfish human nature no longer drives us. "For by these He has granted to us His precious and magnificent promises, in order that by them you might become partakers of the divine nature, having escaped the corruption that is in the world by lust."[7]

That's why I can truthfully say, *I am the new black American man.*

New Purposes. We black men must get away from the condemnation of the devil and turn our negatives into positives. The future is ours, because the "new us" controls our destiny. The Lord blotted out the devil's power, ruined sin's hold on mankind, and held it up for public ridicule.[8] The only power Satan can use against us is deception—lying to us about who we really are.

Practice Forgiveness

We cannot erase history. However, through forgiveness we can erase its scars from our memories. Jesus taught, "And whenever you stand praying, forgive, if you have anything against anyone; so that your Father also who is in heaven may forgive you your transgressions. But if you do not forgive, neither will your Father who is in heaven forgive your transgressions."[9]

I had to meditate on verses like this to renew my mind, or else I could have ended up right back on the streets where God saved me. I had to apply the principles to my life.

The first principle of Christian living is forgiveness. We don't forgive when or because someone says he is sorry. We forgive our oppressors so we can move on and put the past behind us. Unforgiveness binds sin to us, so we must forgive quickly if we're to see a cure to the shocking violence and destruction that fill our city streets. It's not safe for an individual to walk from one block to another in our inner cities, even in my hometown of Baton Rouge.

> *If peace and order are to be restored to our inner cities, black men must be the ones to spearhead it.*

Young black males are the primary victims of this violence, from coast to coast. They're also the largest fatherless segment of our population. God has ordained man to be the head of the family. The splintering of our families—with the tragic loss of so many fathers—has created a society suffering from violence and chaos. Simple logic tells us that if peace and order are to be restored to our inner cities, black men must be the ones to spearhead it. *We are called to be the leaders of our communities.*

Of the 30 million black people in the United States, over 20 million attend Christian churches. We have the potential of being free in God and a witness to the world.

But we can only fulfill God's heavenly purposes when we are born again, which doesn't happen just because we sit in a church pew. After the new birth, hostility, bitterness, and revenge give way to love, compassion, and forgiveness.[10]

With the Holy Spirit's guidance, the minds of African-American men can be liberated from the prisons of the past. This freedom enables us to identify with the country God formed on this land where he brought us. Whatever nation you were born in, God chose your time and place before the foundation of the world.[11] Since that is true, it logically follows that God wanted to have 30 million black people living in the United States in the 1990s, because he had work for them to do. We cannot escape the truth of where and when God has planted us.

Fruits of Freedom

America allows its citizens to enjoy the greatest degree of freedom on earth. This country is where God has placed us, because it has the most opportunity to be an influence to the world. Yet black men as a whole will not identify with the citizenship of this nation and thereby forfeit the opportunities God has for us.

Consider the apostle Paul. He was a righteous man. His country, Rome, was not a righteous nation. Yet Paul used his Roman citizenship to fulfill God's purpose in the midst of evil. He didn't travel the world freely because he was a saint. *Rather, his Roman citizenship was Paul's ticket to fulfill his destiny.*

Jesus taught us to give to government the things that belong to government, and to God the things that belong to God. But he was talking about more than taxes and tithes. The Lord stressed the importance of operating in *citizenship*.

What would happen if millions of black men in this country became Christians first, then Americans? What would happen if African-Americans declared their love for God and for the nation where he placed them? Whatever our standard of living, black men would develop and exhibit unselfish loyalty and benevolent concern for America's well-being. We would assume the office of leadership that God established for us. And we would put our power and economic might to use for God's purposes in our own communities and around this world. Imagine it!

Humanly speaking, this sounds impossible. But when we line up with God, he intervenes supernaturally. He causes women and children to support their godly men, and He honors black men by giving us the ability to bless the inner cities and raise our standard of living—economically, educationally, socially, and spiritually.

Scholars have proved that when true revival hits a community, it brings pride, self-respect, dignity, and integrity into people's hearts. Once that comes, they naturally spearhead campaigns to clean up and rebuild their communities. God causes businesses, industries, and the government to subsidize these campaigns as they see constructive, unified citizens working together. This is happening today in various areas. If we will work together, it will occur on a large scale.

Here's the catch: This great, sweeping revival in black America will not thrive until we become Americans. Why? Because God will not let an illegal alien have a revival! Because of His nature, God honors the laws of the land. He does not stand with lawbreakers. His Word clearly says, "Everyone must submit himself to the governing authorities, for there is no authority except that which God has established."[12]

Become Role Models

We black men must accept our God-given roles as leaders and role models for our wives, children, and youth. We must teach our teenagers to love, protect, and respect this nation. And we must also pray for those in authority.[13]

As black men, our next move in this country is to become *Americans*—not Democrats, Republicans, or Independents, but *Americans*. To do so, we must identify with the spirit of America, as so eloquently spelled out in the Preamble to the Constitution. We are entitled to certain "inalienable rights" because *God* gave them to us. These rights must be accepted by faith.

Black men must develop and proclaim with blazing enthusiasm our love for this nation, its values, and its citizens. From pre-Colonial days, our forefathers played a crucial role in developing this into a strong and productive nation. Today, we must strive to keep it that way, so they will not have worked and died in vain.

Because of the struggles of my forefathers and the everlasting grace of God, I came from a rural town and the degradation of homeless life on the streets to where I am today—a pastor and church founder, radio station owner, and author. God is good. When we live by his principles, we start a whole new life.

The truth is that most black Americans, particularly black men, have cursed the system and rejected this nation. Is it any wonder that God's blessing is not on us or our country? Many black Christians want freedom's blessings, but our hearts cannot let go of the inhumane treatment suffered by our ancestors. As a result, we have taught our young people to feel disfranchised. Partly out of hatred for their situation, they turn to the hopelessness of suicide, drugs, anarchy, and gangs.

When we genuinely forgive the past and teach our young people to love this country and to take pride in it and themselves, we'll see great reductions in drug abuse, violence, and destruction. The change will be natural, because people do not want to kill and destroy that which they love.

Our blueprint for progress comes from the Bible. The ancient Jewish people got their civil rights bill while they were captives of the Babylonian Empire. Living there in exile, the prophet Jeremiah gave his people a word on how to behave themselves. One key to their success was in becoming the peacemakers of the land—in the very nation that enslaved and abused them! Though Jeremiah reminded them of their humiliation, he advised:

> *God wants to use the black man as his vessel of healing, especially to save our own children from destruction.*

- "Build houses and live in them; and plant gardens, and eat their produce."[14] In other words, God told them to become business owners and to control their housing and food supply. They were not to wait for the Babylonian government or any other group to do it.

- "Take wives and become the fathers of sons and daughters, and take wives for your sons and give your daughters to husbands, that they may bear sons and daughters; and multiply there and do not decrease."[15] God told them to strengthen and increase their families and decide how they would live.

- "And seek the welfare of the city where I have sent you into exile, and pray to the LORD on its behalf; for in its welfare you will have welfare."[16] Did you catch the full revelation there? God told captives not to protest against the government but to pray for His blessing over it.

In our own time, we must pray for America's peace and prosperity. Violent crimes cost this nation five hundred billion dollars a year. Our children, black youths, are at the forefront of this destructive hemorrhage. Yet God wants to use the black man as his vessel of healing, especially to save our own children from destruction.

Jeremiah wrote, "'For I know the plans that I have for you,' declares the LORD, 'plans for welfare and not for calamity to give you a future and a hope.'"[17] I see the fulfillment of this verse rapidly coming to pass. Before the dawn of the twenty-first century, I believe black men are going to arise, realizing we are the only ones who can bring peace to our communities and restore our children to order. As this happens, the world will marvel at the power that comes from us collectively. But it starts with one man—each one of us, as we submit to the lordship of Jesus Christ.

See how Pastor Bernard describes what it really means to be a Christian in America today in the next chapter. It's time to rise up, brother, and change your world.

13

THE CULTURE OF CHRISTIANITY

by A. R. Bernard

Soon after Rudolph Giuliani took office as the mayor of New York City in 1994, he made sweeping reductions in the city's clergy liaisons. These offices were designed to maintain lines of communication between government and church leaders. Because of his move, various Christian city officials and pastors met to discuss alternatives for getting the gospel into government.

The government, after all, is merely people. If we can influence those people, we can affect our government. That was our purpose the night we met to air our mutual concerns. But every time someone put out an idea, another person popped up and said, "We can't do that. It's religion."

What? I thought. *The homosexuals can band together, march in parades, register with the city as domestic partners, and flaunt their lifestyle because it's their "culture"? And we can't say a word in public because it's "religion"?*

As the Spirit of God moved inside me, I said, "Something is wrong here. We get rejected because we're a religion, and they get accepted because they're a culture. Either they know something I don't, or we've allowed something to happen. I think we've allowed something to happen. That needs to change."

As Christians, we can no longer allow ourselves to be defined as a religion. We're a culture, a way of life that directs our words and conduct every day.

After that meeting, I studied, prayed, and meditated for weeks on religion, Christianity, and what has happened with these forces in the United States.

Religion comes from a Latin word that means "those activities that bind man into a certain relationship with God." But Christianity is much, much more. In fact, a personal relationship with Jesus Christ is the exact opposite of typical religion. Our activities aren't the issue, our hearts are. Christ's biggest opponents were full of religion. At the end of my study, it became clear: As Christians, we must no longer allow ourselves to be defined as a religion. We're a culture. A religion is a set of beliefs and practices that are used only at certain times—in many cases, just once a week. But a culture is a way of life that directs our words and conduct every day.

Why do I emphasize this distinction? Because Jesus made it clear that religion isn't enough. He told religious folks they needed to be born again. He also called them names like "vipers," "snakes," and "hypocrites." Christ didn't come to bring religion, He came to bring the kingdom of God—a new social order that transcends the divisions and barriers men build to separate themselves from other races, classes, and cultures.

That's a pretty scary idea, particularly when people put it into practice. So often we confuse tradition with Christian ideals, worshiping the ways of our forefathers instead of living as God intended. Jesus introduced a new way of life and thinking that was diametrically opposed to what existed. For example, He taught that we should give away what was rightfully ours and love our enemies. His toughest command for me to obey personally is to turn the other cheek when someone strikes out at me.

Yet in such actions we see the foundation of civilization, which begins where chaos and insecurity end. The first enemy we must overcome to build a civilization is fear. When fear disappears, curiosity and creativity are free to express themselves. Jesus came to free all who were in bondage to the fear of death.[1] And the Bible teaches that God did not give us a spirit of fear, but one of love, power, and a sound mind.[2]

God wants to pour into us the same essence he poured into the first man. Adam became a partaker of God's divine image when God breathed life into him. So it is when Jesus reconciles us to the Father, birthing a new creation.[3]

When Christians come to understand more fully who we are and what we have in Christ, we become dangerous to norms and stereotypes. _I want to be dangerous!_ I want to threaten old, established prejudices, hatreds, and divisions that keep our world in turmoil and prevent God's kingdom of peace from coming to earth!

This is at the heart of Christianity and the reason we must define ourselves as a Christian culture. *Culture* is the integrated system of beliefs, customs, traditions, ideas, and products that constitute the life of a people. When I first learned that, I said, "Hey, Christians have traditions, customs, beliefs, and ideas. We even have products. Just check out the marketplace."

As Christians, we have our own language too. When you're on the job and something bad happens, you may say, "Man, that enemy is after me." The nonbeliever next to you will stare and exclaim, "Enemies? You got enemies?" But any fellow Christian knows exactly what you mean.

When We Lost Our Influence

When we Christians stopped looking at ourselves as a culture we lost our cultural influence, particularly in the 1960s. America's "cultural revolution," brought on through music and drugs, caused a breakdown in faith, morals, and values. While this was happening, we sat back and became religious. And the hypocritical, legalistic, man-made show known as "religion" killed us. We "did our thing" on Sunday but overlooked the truth: *Christianity is a way of life.*

We even let society define us in terms of certain attitudes and actions. So it accepts us when we "love everybody" but warns us not to tell the truth. In its view, we must not term anyone's actions sinful or draw any lines because that's not loving, and, after all, God is love. Well, that's a classic example of a half-truth. Yes, God is loving and merciful. But He also tells us there is right and wrong and that we must confess our sin if we expect His forgiveness. In other words, mercy only follows truth.

After I saw this biblical link between telling the truth and receiving mercy, I told my six sons, "You want mercy when you do wrong? Then you'd better come clean. Don't try to cover up your lies or disobedience and expect me to show you compassion." Sound harsh? No! I patterned my actions as a father after the heavenly Father's. Nobody can shake me by calling me "judgmental" when I follow the Father's words.

Biblical ignorance can be cleverly twisted by people in the world to suit their own purposes. That makes Christians who know the Word dangerous. *Ignorance is the strength of any oppressor.*

Those who oppose Christians on a mixture of religious and racial grounds sneer, "Well, that Bible is the white man's Bible." All I can say, then, is that the white man is going to hell, too, because it says, "For *all* have sinned and fall short of the glory of God."[4]

Changing Our Self-Definition

Adam's self-concept came from his connection with the Lord. So did his strength. God told him to have dominion, to be fruitful and multiply, and Adam knew he could do it. When Adam looked at the world, he wasn't afraid of it, didn't feel inferior to it, and didn't think he was inadequate to deal with it. As long as he was connected to God and defined by him, he could name all the animals and handle a multitude of other tasks. He had control of his world.

Yet the moment he sinned, it lowered his self-esteem, and he was in trouble. The world he once mastered began to master him. The world he once defined now defined him.

This has continued throughout history—the world defining men instead of God defining them. Today we have many men defined by the cocaine that rules their lives and destiny. Others become slaves to fashion, cultural images, money, sex, power, or fame—all fleeting illusions that are ultimately dedicated to their destruction. They are spiritual descendants of Adam and his murderous son Cain, who built a culture that resents God and tries to ignore Him.

When God saw Adam's mistake, He basically said, "I have an answer for that: Jesus Christ. If I can get this man reconnected to me, I can take him back to what I intended him to be and make his world what I intended instead of what it is now."

Because of Adam's sin, the culture that God designed got thrown off track. The civilization that should have come from Adam instead came from his son Cain, a murderer. The rebellious Cain established the first urban living experience. Despite his fallen state, he used the ability within him and led the society as it created industry, metallurgy, agriculture, and even entertainment.

Read about Cain and his descendants. They built a city that had all the equipment built into it. He started a civilization, born of men, that became the pattern for all civilizations. This humanly designed system resents God's rulership and doesn't want to retain him in its knowledge. But when Jesus showed up, he said, "I'm preaching a new kingdom, a new culture, a new social order, a new way of thinking."

Though the gospel is often distorted into a materialistic, feel-good prescription, it is truly good news to everyone, especially the poor. God sent his Living Word, his Son, into the world to heal the destruction of poverty. Those who follow the Word's guidance will find freedom from misery, lack, and the self-

Satan has warred hard against marriage because his objective is to get rid of fathers.

centered life that keeps even materially rich people locked in dungeons of despair.

The Importance of Fathers

Jesus also came working miracles. He fed five thousand with only a few fish and loaves of bread, healed the sick, raised the dead, and cast demons out of the oppressed. But this was not so he could draw attention to Himself. He brought glory to his Father. He operated as a Son in close relationship with his Father. Search the Gospels, particularly John, and see how often Christ talked about his Father. He spoke the pattern: "He works and I work."[5]

This shows us another key to the Christian culture: fathers. Satan has warred hard against marriage because his objective is to get rid of fathers. The deliverance of the family, the society, and the nation rests in the hands of the fathers.

The story of the prodigal son shows the foolishness of those who wander from God the Father. They end up spiritually where the prodigal son landed physically—hungry, destitute, and without hope.

The answer for such troubled souls lies in the prodigal's cry, "How many of my father's hired men have more than enough bread, but I am dying here with hunger! I will get up and go to my father."[6] The son's dignity and self-esteem returned just from thinking about his father, even in the midst of a pigpen. And the same experience will be ours spiritually when we turn back to God.

African-American Value

Our Christian definition of culture must also include the value of African-Americans to this society. That's not just because of the past wounds of slavery, but also because of the voices from white and black communities (plus other ethnic groups) who strive to keep various groups separate when God wants us to come together.

Take one of the labels that some have tried to place on black people—"genetically inferior." For example, a few years ago, the president of Rutgers University touched off a national controversy when he said that disadvantaged students don't score well on college entrance exams because of their heredity. He later apologized and explained that he "misspoke," but there are plenty of folks out there who believe what he first said. Whole books have been written about our alleged genetic inferiority.

Granted, many voices arise to protest such statements, but what about those who take them to heart? The Bible says life and death are in the power of the tongue.[7] If you buy talk of inferiority, you're allowing someone else to define you, to place limitations on you that aren't true, and to bind you up so you'll never reach your maximum potential.

Take heart from David. When he heard about Israel's war with the Philistines and mighty Goliath, it didn't disturb him. In his mind, Israel was winning. Then he took food to his brothers in the trenches, where he saw fear and trembling and heard talk of failure. Even the king huddled in the back, hoping someone else would take on the dreaded task of facing the giant.

This scene didn't square with what David knew about his God. This fear couldn't be from the God who had helped him fight the lion and the bear in the wilderness. This couldn't be that same God's army. So he stood up to face Goliath, believing God alone would give him the victory. He even refused the armor they tried to give him, saying he didn't know how to use that stuff.

If you buy talk of inferiority, you're allowing someone else to define you, to place limitations on you that aren't true, and to bind you up so you'll never reach your maximum potential.

When Goliath cursed this little shepherd boy, David replied, "This day the LORD will deliver you up into my hands, and I will strike you down and remove your head from you. And I will give the dead bodies of the army of the Philistines this day to the birds of the sky and the wild beasts of the earth, that all the earth may know that there is a God in Israel."[8] What faith!

The same kind of faith in God and his Son, Jesus Christ, will motivate you to great feats. Like David and his slingshot, your greatest strength is always what you know and have, not what others know or have. Armed only with what God has given you, you can have faith for great works. That faith gives you a belief that he can lift you above obstacles and conquer enemies that look bigger than Goliath.

This courageous vision will send you to the homeless man to say, "That's not you. You've become somebody else. Let me tell you who you really are." Or it will send you to the prostitute, whom you can encourage, "Who told you this is the only way you can survive? Who told you the only value you have is your sex? I've got a gospel to preach to you that will bring you back to the original beauty God intended for you."

That's our Christian culture—one of promise, fulfillment, and hope. Go back to the Beginner of life and let Him rule your life. Then proclaim that you're part of the Christian culture. It's not just a religion, but the way to the peaceful civilization the world is dying to see.

▲ ▲ ▲ ▲ ▲

Your greatest strength is always what you know and have. Armed only with what God has given you, you can have faith for great works.

▼ ▼ ▼ ▼ ▼

To impact our culture, we need men who will fulfill their God-given responsibility to be leaders in the home, community, and nation. My friend A.C. Green, the basketball star, is going to get you started in leadership in the next chapter.

Part Six

RESTORING MEN TO LEADERSHIP

If you pay attention to the commands of the LORD your God that I give you this day and carefully follow them, you will always be at the top, never at the bottom.

Deuteronomy 28:13 NIV

14

LEADERSHIP 101

by A.C. Green

My first two years in college, I took a lot of classes with the course number 101, like History 101 and English 101. Those were introductory classes I had to pass in order to go on to more advanced subjects. Academics didn't come easy to me, not compared to sports anyway, and I worked hard to learn the basics so I could move ahead.

In leadership, there are also basics we have to learn to move on, and they may not come easily to us at first. We have to master certain beginning-level skills before God can use us in more important matters. The Lord instructs us to master sin.[1] He wants us to master skills as well, so we are not at the mercy of sin or ignorance. Often I see men trying to start out in leadership on a 201 level, attempting to climb the ladder without using the first rung, and they fall flat on their faces. There are no shortcuts in fulfilling God's plan for our lives.

The first thing to learn in leadership is that you can't be a leader until you learn to follow one. The principle is simple: *Find a leader and follow the leader.*

The second principle is teamwork. There are no "lone ranger" Christians. Fulfilling God's purposes in our lives takes help from others. God brings us into relationships with other believers who form our inner circle, our core team. _Men don't win without a team. Teams don't win without committed men._

▲ ▲ ▲ ▲ ▲

Find a leader and follow the leader.

▼ ▼ ▼ ▼ ▼

Let me explain this with some examples from my own life. At the end of a recent basketball season, my former team, the Phoenix Suns, was favored to go all the way and win the finals. Going into the play-offs, we had to pull our heads out of the clouds and not take any wins for granted. Our first-round opponent was the Portland Trail Blazers, and they were seriously gunning for us.

After putting them down in game one, our second game against them came up on national television as the third part of a triple-header. In the first two games that day, the teams favored to win had lost miserably. We all saw the reports and knew we could be served our heads on platters too.

Our team captains, Charles Barkley and Kevin Johnson, encouraged us by saying we couldn't rely on what we did two days before. In his closing pep talk before taking the floor, Kevin said, "We have to come out and be stronger, more committed, more focused. This is the toughest game."

Charles closed with, "We need to rebound, play solid defense, and come out with enthusiasm and life."

We came out fighting, quickly racked up some points, and were off to a good start.

The Bible says, "Five of you will chase a hundred, and a hundred of you will chase ten thousand."[2] It's amazing that when we work together, our teammates don't just *add* to our effectiveness; they *multiply* what we can do on our own.

This is such a powerful principle—on the basketball court, at church, and on a personal level. When we pull together, the job can be accomplished, and we can reach our goals. The problem is that the devil knows this also. When it comes to the serious matters in life, like our Christian faith, he'll scratch and claw to keep us from supporting one another, to get us alone so he can knock us off.

My team captains hit on another core principle that day: *The greater commitment we have to our purpose, the greater our resolve must be.* Think about that one. When we're committed to win, we can't let little pitfalls

Fulfilling God's purposes in our lives takes help from others.

stop us. When we're committed to becoming the men God wants us to be, we can't beat ourselves up over faltering or falling into sin. We must be resolved that regardless of what happens, we'll never stop repenting, never stop praying, never stop pressing toward our purpose in Christ.

There is one voice, one call, one focus of our faith, and that's Jesus. And although we differ individually, we arrive at our goals and purposes together, as a team.

During every game of my basketball season, I have to put these principles into practice. The coaches appoint team captains at the beginning of the season. That year, ours were Kevin and Charles.

Now, Charles Barkley and I are close to the same height, so we can look each other in the eye. But other than that, Charles and I rarely see eye to eye. If I wanted to, I could be very uncomfortable with his leadership on my team. But more important matters concern me— namely, winning. For a man to be able to win, he has to follow the leadership that's given to him. If I don't submit to Charles's leadership, I can ruin my own chances and potentially stop the whole team from reaching its goals.

When Charles gives his final pregame pep talk before we approach the court, I choose to submit to his direction and advice for two reasons: (1) He's the captain, and (2) a team divided against itself will not win consistently.

I put aside my personal differences and ideologies for the sake of a bigger purpose. This should sound familiar to churchgoing people. It's especially true when it comes to following a pastor. We have to set aside our personal differences for the sake of Christ's call on our lives— the bigger purpose.

On the day of that big game, with Charles's words ringing in my ears, I went out on the court and did exactly what he said. I rebounded ferociously, elbows flying as I landed. I slam-dunked the ball over my opponent's head just to intimidate him. I was all over that court like a madman. I knew that if I would follow the leader, our team had a good chance of winning.

What I didn't know was that while I was giving it my all, one television announcer was saying I was as dirty a player as the infamous Rick Mahorn, but that since I was a nice guy, I didn't have his reputation. From what my friends told me later, the announcer never let up on me through that whole game.

That brings up another crucial principle of leadership: *God is the only one whose approval we need.* We don't have to worry about what others say as long as our Father says, "Well done."

Among men, especially in the black community, I've noticed a strong need for approval and validation from other men. Men tend to say things like, "I started this program," "I led this ministry," or "I'm the reason this business is growing." We say such things only because we desire approval from the wrong team captain—man, not God.

Our identity isn't in how big our church is, how much money we have, or how many people we influence. Instead, we find our identity in Christ and in what the Spirit has called us to do. We're ultimately on God's team, not man's.

If our church reaches one hundred people in our community, great; we commit to that purpose. If a neighboring church grows to one thousand, great; they commit to their purpose. One is no greater than the other, as long as we're each doing our part within the body of Christ. *Let's save our friendly competition for the basketball court or playing field and get it out of our walk with Christ.*

God is the only one whose approval we need.

In my neighborhood growing up, there was always competition in material things between kids and between parents. We loved to show off our bikes, cars, clothes, and vacation plans. Even at school, we had "show-and-tell," where we could flaunt whatever we had or did.

▲ ▲ ▲ ▲ ▲

We unquestionably accomplish much more when we pull together than we do when we pull apart.

▼ ▼ ▼ ▼ ▼

When we become Christians and receive blessings from our good Father, we often talk about them in the same old way, like "show-and-tell." We muddle the spiritual goal, which is to give glory to God, with the fleshly nature, which wants the glory for ourselves.

Such competition destroys the bond of unity in God's team. Comparing ourselves to others creates problems with self-esteem too. If you don't compare yourself to others, you won't feel inferior to anyone.

Such competition also creates an inability to submit to authority. We feel that if we can't be the top dog, we won't be a dog at all. Then we pull away from others—usually the very people God set in our path to help us reach our goals. These brothers and sisters in Christ would encourage us and rejoice with us in our accomplishments if we let them. But instead we cut ourselves off.

And once we've separated ourselves from other believers—well, it would be like me taking on the Chicago Bulls all alone and expecting to win. In a word, it's stupid. In the same way, you don't want to take on the devil alone. You need your team behind you, that smaller group of people God has brought into your life who really know you and are *for* you. *We unquestionably accomplish much more when we pull together than we do when we pull apart.*

In that game against the Trail Blazers, the Suns fought valiantly as a team, and we achieved our goal—we won. Oddly enough, the same announcer who called me "dirty" started to sing my praises in the end. Some fans and local radio deejays helped him see the light. For some reason, the announcers continued to praise me throughout the play-off season. I did the same things I'd always done, but the winds in the announcer's booth had changed. That's one more reason not to look for approval in others: People change, but God never changes.

The final game of that series was at the old Municipal Auditorium in Portland. I was raised in Portland. This was the same court where I'd won the state high school championship fifteen years earlier. It was also the same court where I'd played often in college. And it was the same court where I'd first played professional basketball in front of my old friends, with my new teammates Kareem Abdul-Jabbar and Magic Johnson—and shot a brick out of nervousness. The place was full of memories.

That day was to be the last time the old auditorium would be used for professional basketball. Although the home fans wanted their team to win, they acknowledged that I was their homeboy. I wanted to win one last time in that familiar setting, and so did my teammates. As we pulled together, combining our strengths unselfishly, we did just that.

To win spiritually, we need to find that core team that will help us achieve our goals. God always starts right where we are. He'll bring men into our lives with whom we learn how to build, fall, struggle, and grow together. Those friendships become our championship team. _The closer the relationship we allow God to build for us with a handful of fellow Christians, the better and more effective our Christian walk will become._

On God's team today, we need men who have learned to be solid leaders—ones who are not afraid to claim the words of the apostle Paul when he said, "Follow my example, just as I follow Christ's."[3] We need men who, without shrinking back, are willing to take the responsibility that comes along with that claim. We need men who will adopt humility, a servant's attitude, and who are as willing to follow as they are to lead.

Jesus will give you as many precious jewels as he can trust you with. If you have children, those are the first ones you lead. As you're trustworthy with them, God will give you other places of leadership. Paul told Timothy, "And the things which you have heard from me in the presence of many witnesses, these entrust to faithful men, who will be able to teach others also."[4]

> **The closer the relationship we allow God to build for us with a handful of fellow Christians, the better, more effective our Christian walk will become.**

Leaders must keep a close relationship with the Father. Jesus said His desire was for us to _know_ his Father. I _know of_ my team's fans, but I _know_ my teammates. Because of our daily activities, I understand them and their tendencies—who's a morning person and who's moody before lunch. In the same way, we get to know God by spending time with Him.

It's vital that we master these basics. To follow God often means to follow the leaders he brings into our lives. The more we become submissive and accountable to those God has placed in authority, the easier it is for the Holy Spirit to flow through us and for us to flow with Him.

Get on the team, start with the basics, and practice, practice, practice. Every man was created to be a leader. I started out as a shy kid from Portland; but by teaching me the basics, God has made me a leader. He'll make you one too.

For a hint of what advanced leadership is all about, read the last two chapters. In them, a couple of men who have led hundreds of men are going to tell you their secrets of leadership. If you'll follow the leader, you can become a leader as well.

15

BUILDING A CHURCH WITH MEN

by James Meeks

To lead men, you have to learn what makes them tick. Ever hear the story about the 350-pound man swimming at a resort lake when stomach cramps struck him? Suddenly he dropped under the water. On shore, a champion swimmer who weighed a mere 100 pounds watched the man sinking. Others who knew of the champion's talents cried, "Hey! Don't you see that man drowning?"

"Yes," he said quietly.

"Why don't you go out there and save him?"

"I will."

Just then, the huge man poked his head above the surface, gulped a mouthful of water as he thrashed about, and yelled, "Help! Help!"

The little man stood calmly, digging his toes into the sand as he stood silently with his arms folded to his chest.

"Man, hurry up!" people in the crowd urged. "That guy's going to die! He's drowning, man. Why are you just standing there watching him?"

"I'll get him," the champion swimmer said, not moving.

The big man resurfaced, kicking and screaming, frantically clinging to life. "Help! Help!"

"Man, listen, if this guy dies, it's going to be your fault," accused a man in the crowd. "It's going to be in the headlines: 'Champion Swimmer Watches Man Drown.'"

"I'll get him."

Just then, the drowning man collapsed and sank under the water for the third time. The waves stirred by his panic-driven paddling softened to ripples.

Splash! The champion swimmer hit the water. In what seemed like a few seconds, he had reached the victim, pulled his head above the water, and smoothly glided with him back to the shore. The 350-pounder stumbled onto the beach and sank to his knees, coughing and gulping air.

"Man, why did you wait so long?" several people exclaimed, eyebrows arched high. "You could have saved that guy five or six minutes ago."

"No, I couldn't," the champion told them. "Six minutes ago, he had a whole lot of fight left in him. If I had dived in then, he would have pulled both of us under the water and drowned me with him. I just had to wait until all his fight disappeared. Then I was able to jump in and save him."

That's a great example of how God treats us. He waits until we've done everything we know how to do, and then he rescues us. He waits until we try all the special conferences, seminars, church growth plans, and sink-or-swim strategies and give up in disgust, unable to wave our arms any longer. Then he steps in to bring what we were seeking the whole time.

Want to see men assuming their rightful roles as spiritual leaders, strong fathers, faithful husbands, and servants? The answer is simply to pray. Men come from God. The church that wants to grow will only do so when it attracts men, and nothing draws men more quickly or easily than a praying church. Only when we pray does heaven get busy.

Seeking Men

Salem Baptist Church started ten years ago in a small day-care center with barely over a dozen men. Today we have more than 1,000 strong, Godly men. There are more men in our Sunday school and Wednesday night services than in any other church in Chicago. Most of them were prayed in.

The church that wants to grow will only do so when it attracts men, and nothing draws men more quickly or easily than a praying church.

Like most churches, when we started we had a majority of women. But every Sunday I prayed, "God, we need you to send men." When men walked the aisles to accept Christ as their Savior, the whole church stood up triumphantly, praising the Lord for answering our prayers. Nobody resented me leading these prayers for men or how I admired, applauded, and praised them.

A pastor who is afraid of women can never "grow" a church. A pastor who is afraid to talk about the biblical position of men and how God created them to lead will never see men rise up and lead. Aware of this, I became the head cheerleader for our men. I stood them up and praised them constantly: "Look at these good-looking, strong brothers. Here are men who work hard. They're good family men who need your prayers. They need to be lifted up and know that somebody cares about them."

> **Every real man should take leadership in the church and in his home, because God designed him to be in charge.**

Our world has tilted off track so badly that many men are afraid to stand up and _be_ men. But every real man should take leadership in the church and in his home, because God designed him to be in charge. This is more than a lofty theory. We can and must put it into practice.

Once a woman in the congregation came to me and said, "Pastor, my husband wants me to go somewhere else with him next Sunday. He doesn't want me to come to church. He's always complaining, 'All you do is go down to that church all the time. You need to go somewhere with me once in a while.'"

"Go on, go with him," I told her. "And when he asks you what's happening, tell him your pastor said he's the leader, and you're not going to be a fussy wife. You're going to be submissive and do what he wants to do."

The next Saturday night, she told her husband, "Honey, tomorrow, wherever it is you've been wanting me to go, I'm going to go with you. My pastor said you're the head of the household, and I'm to be submissive to you and follow you."

Sunday morning, he arose first and got dressed. Puzzled, his wife said, "Honey, I thought you said the thing we were going to didn't start until noon. It's only ten o'clock. What are you doing?"

"We're going to church," he replied.

"What do you mean? Why are we going to church?"

"Because," he said, "I want to see that man who had enough sense to tell you that I'm supposed to be in charge."

Men need empowerment. They need pastors who are willing to stand up for them, understand their nature, and reinforce them to meet their awesome responsibilities. I do everything I can to serve men and not place myself above them. A pastor can't sit on his throne like King Tut and accept accolades and praise and never give any honor to his congregation.

Once men discover the pastor isn't out for himself, there's nothing they won't do for him or the church.

For a long time, I wouldn't drive a new car because none of my men owned one. I could have easily done so. As fast as our church was growing, I could have bought a top-of-the-line model.

But I wanted to attract men, and to do that I had to forgo my personal desires.

One day, however, when our battered old car was smoking again, one of my men came to me and said, "Now listen, you're either going to get a car, or we're going to go get you a car, or else we're going to get rid of you. You won't embarrass us any longer!" That came from the congregation, not me. Once men discover the pastor isn't out for himself, there's nothing they won't do for him or the church.

Logical People

Thanks to prayer and some biblically based teaching, I grasped a key truth about dealing with men. I saw that they can't be led by their emotions. Men and women as a general rule have their strengths in different sides of their natures: Men respond from their "thinking" side and women from their "feeling" side.

Women's emotional strength allows them to provide nurture and gives a deep-seated intuition that lets them know, for instance, if someone is a bad apple because "he just doesn't feel right."

Men are generally more analytical and goal oriented. Most men can tell you every player's height and weight on their favorite football team, why the team is struggling, and what it will take to turn things around. Men sit in a barbershop and talk about who won the heavyweight championship in 1947 and who's the greatest boxer of all time.

But faith doesn't appeal to logic. What kind of logic says, "Love those who hate you" and "You get by giving"? The way to reach men is to teach them. They can't be sung to, screamed at, or whooped into heaven; men need to understand the Manual. A man who reads manuals can put together anything, whether it's a model car, a boat, or a house. He just needs the ABCs in straight order.

So logical, expository preaching is necessary in teaching the gospel. At my church, we start at Genesis chapter 1, verse 1, and then go to verse 2, then 3, 4, and straight down through the whole chapter. Then the rest of the book. Men can follow that and deal with it. It's an orderly approach that feels comfortable. If you're just starting your Christian walk, I encourage you to get some teaching materials like that, starting your study with the Gospels in the New Testament.

> *The way to reach men is to teach them. They can't be sung to, screamed at, or whooped into heaven; men need to understand the Manual.*

Once a man gets through enough books to grasp hold of the truth, he'll start shouting, because he'll understand Christians have something to shout about. It reminds me of the old saying: "Good meat makes its own gravy." Everything else will follow the study of the Word. That's why Paul told Timothy, "Preach the word."[1] Not preach the news, the latest trend, or your feelings. *Preach the Word.*

Men need to be taught to give too. Ultimately, giving to the Lord's work is a matter of faith, which is why men must grasp the concept and respond at their own pace. Try to get it any other way and you're asking for trouble, because most men don't respond to passing the plate. You know: "Well, we're going to take an offering for the roof. Now one for the windows. Well, pastor's going to the convention, and he needs some extra funds."

If you want to reach men, the men you already know are the best tool.

If a church is going to grow, I believe it ought to grow on regular tithes and offerings. That's a dangerous stand for most preachers, because it goes against our grain. It's in our blood to make inspirational appeals, because we yearn to see the Lord's work carried out. But years ago, when I decided to stop taking extra offerings, it worked. No longer could members use the excuse, "I can't tithe, because by the time I give my dues here, for men's day over there, and then for the building fund, there's nothing left."

Men Are Goal Oriented

If you want to provoke some laughter, ask an unsaved man to come to Sunday school. Or ask a male member of your church how much he enjoys his class. One day I walked into our men's Sunday school class (we separate the men from the women). There were about fifteen in the group. Shaking my head, I said, "God, something has to give."

Although I don't have anything against them, we quit using quarterly lesson books. Why? Because men need to talk about issues that involve and affect them. I went out and bought Edwin Louis Cole's *Maximized Manhood* and started teaching from it. After that, we started going through *Communication, Sex and Money*, also by Ed Cole.[2]

After a while we had twenty-five men in class. Then a few more started filtering in as word spread about this interesting class. But I knew that men are goal oriented and love to be challenged. To stir things up, I went to the women and said, "I'll bet you we can have sixty-five men in Sunday school next Sunday."

They had never seen more than thirty, so they said, "Bet you can't."

I replied, "OK, if we do, you have to fix breakfast for us."

Then I went back to the men and said, "We're going to have sixty-five men if we have to grab a few from the mental hospital, take some guys on a weekend pass from jail, and retrieve some prisoners with those monitoring devices on their legs." The next Sunday, we had seventy-five men. Then we issued a challenge to take it up to 125. Now we have a dozen times more.

There are two key points to this story:

1. *Men are different from women.* When a man gets up to go to church, the whole house is going too! You get a man excited about coming to a church where he can talk about issues affecting his life, and he'll be charging around the house, commanding, "Get up from there! Let's go! It's time for Sunday school!"

2. *Don't be afraid to have contests and goals.* People think that isn't biblical, but consider the parable Jesus told about a man who had been stealing from his boss and was going to lose his job. He went around to everyone who owed his master money and marked down their accounts, accepting 20 percent less from one man and 50 percent less from another. Then, when he lost his job, he had someone to go back to and ask for a favor. Jesus commended the dishonest man, saying the children of darkness are wiser than Christians in their plans.[3]

Do you think people in the world sponsor wet T-shirt contests and bikini contests and big leg contests and panty hose contests just for the fun of it? No! They know such things attract people. I definitely don't mean churches should sponsor wet T-shirt contests. But there's nothing wrong with setting a goal to see how many men can bring other men to services—as long as you don't do gimmicks *instead of* prayer.

We hold these events to inspire our members. For example, sometimes we offer men free dinner (for them and their wives) if they bring twenty or more men to church. Once we had a Sunday school promotion in which we offered a free cruise to the person who brought the most guests.

"Well, you're just bribing people to come to church!" some say. But if we see more than one thousand new faces on a Sunday and several hundred of them get saved, how much is that worth? I don't care how many cruises we give away when we see those results.

Teaching Men to Lead by Serving

Once you tap into the male, goal-oriented outlook, you're ready to organize men to lead. I started with fifteen willing men and spent two years teaching them every Friday morning. We met at 6:00 A.M. for a ninety-minute class, and I poured my life into them. I taught them everything I knew about God's Word and ways and how He created them to be leaders.

The men responded. After these classes began, those fifteen men started showing up early on Sunday mornings to serve. They would stand out in front of the church, ready to meet needs. When people drove up, here were our men, looking good in their suits, carrying umbrellas if it was raining, helping women to the door, carrying children across the street, and parking cars. Not a man was inside, but when people drove up, they exclaimed, "Oh, look at all the men in that church!"

Though few in number, those men pursued other men. When a guy dropped off his wife, they flagged him down to ask, "Hey, where are you going? Pull over, pull over, man, let's talk. Why are you just dropping off your wife? Don't you know she and the children need you here? You know, the family that prays together stays together."

Often, these men protested, "There ain't nothin' in there but y'all preacher men, all dressed up."

Eventually we changed from wearing Sunday suits to wearing jogging suits so the men out front could say, "No, man! What you're wearing is fine. Come on, park the car. Come inside, and I'll show you my pastor." And when they pointed me out, these guys' eyes would bug out. "That's your preacher?"

Thank goodness we realized that church wasn't designed to be a fashion show, and we quit worrying about how people were dressed. One Sunday, even the Good Humor man slid in the back door and got saved.

When I preached his funeral, I thanked God from my heart that he had gone to heaven. He might be in hell today if we had continued to emphasize clothes.

If you want to reach men, the men you already know are the best tool. All of our trained men are leaders now. They lead by serving. We have the "New Testament Program," so called because we name each zip code area where our members live after a New Testament book. Various deacons and assistant pastors oversee each area, with fifteen men under them. Each of those fifteen men is responsible for ten families.

That means when someone gets sick, you call the man. When somebody dies, you report it to the man. If a member's utilities get cut off or his child gets in trouble, the man comes. When someone goes to the hospital, men come and tend to them. They walk into the sick person's room and say, "We're here on behalf of the pastor. He sent us to find out what you need."

These men aren't working just to make me look good. Their primary purpose is to *serve*. They serve the congregation so that I can devote more of my time to preaching and teaching. This is the model outlined in Acts 6, when the apostles appointed deacons to serve the church so they (the apostles) could concentrate on spreading the gospel.

When men have responsibility, they respond. If you challenge men with something to do, your church or men's group will flower and grow in ways you never thought possible. But don't try it by simply drawing up a pattern based on what we're doing or what someone across town tried. Pray! Then act as God brings in the men.

The patterns God gives us are unique to our calling and circumstances, but his principles remain the same. The next chapter will show you how Pastor Gilbert Thompson in Boston used the same principles and arrived at the same goals, but through a totally different pattern.

16

A CHURCH WITHOUT WALLS

by Gilbert Thompson

Boston is a tough place to plant a church. I moved here to pastor what was at the time New England's largest congregation in our denomination, and it had only sixty members. Big-name preachers would visit New England and shake the dust off their shoes as they left. Statistics show just 10 percent of the population regularly attends church.

Yet, God has built a strong congregation, having a healthy percentage of men, in this hostile environment. I now see light shining in dark places, and I'm seeing inner-city men being transformed into strong leaders in their homes, church, and community. This miracle in Boston came from society's seemingly most powerless members—black inner-city men.

Before I started using God's pattern, I thought of trying all kinds of gimmicks to attract crowds. There was the banana gimmick: "Bring a bunch to church;" the family and friends approach: "Y'all bring everyone you know"; and the open invitation: "Just bring somebody." But despite growth that impressed many colleagues, nothing seemed to make a permanent impact. For every three steps forward, we slid back two.

Upsetting? Naturally. After all, I was doing things "the right way," and I had credentials. After a year at Northwestern University's Garrett Theological Seminary, I enrolled in Boston University's School of Theology, where I completed my degree. In those days, I pastored a church that grew from sixty to four hundred in ten years. Some said, "You should be happy," but I knew there was more.

When I left that congregation to start a new church, I had much to learn. The answers I needed came from the obvious cornerstone of a Christian's life—prayer. One day as I agonized over my desire to see lasting, life-changing growth in our new church, New Covenant Christian Center, the Lord sparked a thought in my mind: *You don't pray enough, son.*

Immediately I saw how careless I was about my prayer life. I could hear him in my spirit, softly saying, You don't treat your time with me as if it's important. *You set a time with me, but anybody can take my time. I want you to make an appointment that you keep. If you have a dentist's appointment, you make it. If you have a plane to catch, you get there early. I want you to meet with me and get there early. If you want to grow, you have to pray.*

So I prayed. It took years to do it consistently. I would be faithful, slip up, then resume. But God strengthened my grip on this discipline with a promise: *If you will make prayer your priority, I will establish spiritual prosperity to the next generation.* I learned that through prayer, God's anointing can touch an entire congregation.

Prayer gave focus to New Covenant. A few months after we began, church leaders gathered in our home to discuss personal and ministry concerns. After lengthy conversation we decided to seek God's answers to our problems.

We prayed, and the Lord's presence filled the room. I felt the Holy Spirit take over my personal prayer. Though I couldn't grasp what was happening, I continued, believing he would bring an understanding of his message. I waited quietly and asked, "Lord, what does this mean?" Suddenly these words came to me: *A church without walls.*

Breaking out of the Walls

That phrase reminded me of the prophet Zechariah, who said, "'Jerusalem will be inhabited without walls, because of the multitude of men and cattle within it. For I,' declares the LORD, 'will be a wall of fire around her, and I will be the glory in her midst.'"[1]

I realized that a great deal of my frustration stemmed from working within a traditional church structure. I had to begin anew, building New Covenant according to God's patterns and principles. As I meditated on His Word, the Lord showed me how to establish a church whose spiritual and numerical growth did not depend on a building but on the multiplication of discipled men. An inner-city ministry centered on a physical location always faces two major problems: lack of inspiration and lack of space.

Lack of Inspiration

The ghetto, especially an economically depressed ghetto, can stifle a pastor's spirit. A building cannot be the source of inspiration for him or the church's spirit and vision. Inner-city churches seldom boast of grand temples or cathedrals with spires and towers. We cannot allow the physical building to hold our inspiration hostage. The structure is not the church.

Lack of Space.

Potential varies according to geographical location. In the suburbs, a growing church usually has an availability of land to expand, but not so with an inner-city congregation. Its building may be boxed in. The surrounding property may not be available or too expensive to purchase. Pastors and congregations who limit their vision to a particular building or area may limit their potential for growth.

God showed me to structure a ministry that would concentrate on discipling men. Not that we don't have a building. But we have three times as many members as the sanctuary holds, and we aren't worried. Here are three areas of focus in our discipling:

1. *Men of Faith:* Our vision was first to produce men of faith.
2. *Men of Strength:* Once we grasped the power and ability of God by faith, we strove to produce men of strength.
3. *Men of Mission:* Out of faith and strength naturally arises the third element, men of mission.

People need to see the church, the kingdom of God, in real life—in their neighborhoods, grocery stores, and places of work. They need to see God walking on earth, which happens through his children speaking, teaching, and acting on his truth.

We teach that you must say what you hear, so that you can see what you say. We encourage our men to seek God's face for a "word" of his will for their lives. When they hear that "word," we encourage them to believe it and speak it. Those faith-filled words, fitly spoken, form the

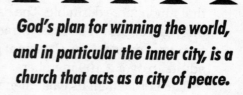

God's plan for winning the world, and in particular the inner city, is a church that acts as a city of peace.

foundation for the miracle of God's movement in their circumstance.

Men of Faith

God called us to build a church that established men of faith: "Jerusalem will be inhabited without walls, because of the multitude of men."[2]

In the Bible, Jerusalem is the city where God lives. The name Jerusalem means "city of peace." The phrase "a city without walls" means a place with no boundaries. A "multitude of men" refers to growth and development. The meaning is clear—when God is allowed to live and operate in an atmosphere of peace where there are no man-made boundaries or limitations, growth will be the result.

God's plan for winning the world, and in particular the inner city, is a church that acts as a city of peace. Old Testament Jerusalem foreshadowed the New Testament church as the city of God. Jesus called us "a city set on a hill" that can't be hidden.[3] The church is also identified as heavenly Jerusalem.[4]

Our church has experienced remarkable success in communicating this peace. In spite of Boston's turmoil and trouble, men come. Desperate conditions make God that much more desirable. The darker it gets, the brighter our light shines. The light attracts men. During a fourteen-year period, New Covenant grew from less than 100 adults to over 2,100 members.

The Lord taught us what men need to *know*. In an area many in the world label "hopeless," we teach that God has given us hope when we know we are in Christ. God promises us both a hope and a future.[5] He says the earth will eventually be filled with the knowledge of God's glory, just as the waters cover the sea.[6] We don't live in fear, because the Father has been pleased to give us the kingdom.[7] Because we believe in God's promises, we look forward to seeing his kingdom in all its power and blessings.

Men who are planted in the seedbed of truth experientially, also know great growth. Take the young man of seventeen who came to Boston to attend the Massachusetts Institute of Technology in the mid-1970s. A new Christian, he joined our church and began to flower as the Word of God took root in his spirit. He witnessed on college campuses, won many to Christ, and accepted a call to preach. Courtney's first sermon was to our people, and he now pastors a thriving church in Virginia.

Knowledge of the truth produces men of faith. Jesus told us that if we hold to His truth, we become his disciples and gain our freedom.[8] Men most easily grasp truth when it's presented in an orderly, systematic fashion. There are five foundational, progressive levels on which we build strong lives. As you grow in Christ and in leadership, I recommend these five steps:

1. Christ. A new believer must come to a knowledge of Christ. He seeks to answer the questions: "Who is Christ?" "What did Christ do?" and "How do I make Christ Lord?" This practical, experiential learning leads to assurance of salvation. We teach it in our foundations class.

2. Word. After a man grasps this foundation and can confess, "I am standing as a new creation in Christ," growth in understanding becomes all-important. The Bible is that food, the Word of God, and a trustworthy source for spiritual nourishment.

The historical accuracy and spiritual reliability of Scripture is vital to inner-city ministry, particularly in an age when so many scholars attack the Bible's accuracy and authority. Besides its truth, the new believer must grasp the principles of observation, interpretation, and application to his life. With this foundation stone in place, he is able to confess, "I am walking in obedience."

3. Prayer. Prayer is pivotal in spiritual development. It's vital to our abiding in Christ and walking in obedience. We emphasize the Lord's Prayer as Jesus' preferred prayer outline. Prayer is an underused tool in the church. A new believer must become a praying believer so that when trouble comes, he is able to pray himself through. The confession of men grounded in the foundation stone of prayer is, "We are communing in God's presence."

4. Fellowship. After a man knows how to commune with God, he's ready for fellowship, a spiritual by-product of praying for and with others. The Lord designed believers for fellowship. This is a powerful truth in modern society, where selfishness reigns and most will only "look out for number one." By standing together, we develop a spirit of cooperation. It is no longer "dog-eat-dog" but "brother-keep-brother."

Fellowship comes from the pillars of _faith_, _hope_, and _love_. Faith answers the questions of who we are in Christ and what we believe. It also enables us to identify with other faithful Christians in the midst of cults and confusion. Hope tells us what we have in Christ—our perspective, dreams, and potential, and how we can live in unity. The power of love shows us that all things are possible in Christ as we look to the future. The confession of men grounded in the foundation stone of fellowship is, "We are sharing in covenant."

> **_By standing together, we develop a spirit of cooperation. It is no longer "dog-eat-dog," but "brother-keep-brother."_**

5. Witnessing. Finally, we teach witnessing. As men experience fellowship, they realize there are many who still need this joy. Witnessing is not motivated by fear or guilt but by love. The emphasis is simply the good news that Jesus died on the cross and rose from the dead to open the door for sinners to enter God's kingdom. As bold men of faith, we confess, "We are serving in ministry."

Men of Strength

Men of strength are another key element and for a crucial reason: *Men cannot become strong without surviving difficulties.* Men of strength are made, not born. In many respects, the church of the late twentieth century fails to develop men of strength because it doesn't take full advantage of the supernatural, enabling Holy Spirit. He surrounds, protects, and empowers us as we learn how to pray.

"'For I,' declares the LORD, 'will be a wall of fire around her.'"[9] God's protection surrounds those grounded in the truth. His supernatural presence is essential to every inner-city ministry. God is a wall of fire, the protection believers need. Men must be introduced to the power and ministry of the Holy Spirit, made available through prayer.

Men of strength understand that walking in God's anointing is a lifestyle, that God reigns in the earth through them. Strength attracts men, and strong men attract other men.

The power of the Holy Spirit is part of our strategy for reaching men. Through the clarity of his message and his power, we are more skilled at pulling Satan's blindfolds off men's minds.[10] They begin to see the truth behind Satan and his deceptive work.

The Holy Spirit's powerful deliverance ministry can make old things new. Such was the case with Doug, a church member who was saved in prison after more then twenty years of heroin addiction. He's now happily married, works as a chemical clinician in the court system, and oversees our substance abuse ministry. We've seen many others develop similar fruitfulness.

The strength created by this life-changing, revealing Holy Spirit power has produced what I call an "empowerment reality." That's when men understand God's dominion power in everyday life. One of the primary ways this occurs is through continuing in prayer. We hold prayer meetings from 5:00 to 7:00 A.M. each weekday and from 7:00 to 8:30 A.M. on Saturdays.

This initiative has spurred supernatural occurrences for which there are no adequate human explanations. Among other things, we have seen:

- Dramatic increases in both numbers and the quality of our members' spiritual understanding.
- Answers to prayers for healing and deliverance on a weekly basis.
- God raising up prayer warriors who stand with me.

A young man of God, Pastor Roland, developed into a great intercessor and saw his wife delivered from the enemy's oppression and most of his family members saved. He has an ever-increasing ministry to the people of Boston.

Prayer gives a greater sense of power and purpose in five specific areas:

1. Spiritual Perspective. Through the discipline of prayer, men grasp their responsibility to be spiritual leaders and priests at home. They love their wives and lovingly nurture, discipline, and protect their children. The prayer covering of these men builds a wall of fire around their families.

2. *Economic Strength.* Through prayer, men of means and investment acumen have come to understand a principle of prosperity: God gives us the strength to gain wealth in order to confirm His covenant.[11] In addition, as men learn about business and how money works, and as they answer God's call to excellence, they rise in character, commitment, and the wise use of economic power. Many hairdressers, plumbers, and entrepreneurs who make a good living testify that God, through prayer, has raised them up.

> *In a world dominated by racism and discrimination, through prayer, men begin to exhibit unity and peace.*

3. *Social Ministry.* Through prayer, social work becomes a ministry. Men of God must begin to feed, house, clothe, tutor, visit, and counsel people. Ministering to other men's physical and psychological needs is a priority. Hal was saved through a prison ministry. After his release and a brief period of homelessness, he now feeds the homeless and is a part of our growing outreach to the city's disfranchised citizens. Prayer is the beginning of destroying these kinds of social strongholds.

4. *Political Involvement.* "The kingdom of the world has become the kingdom of our Lord, and of His Christ;

and He will reign forever and ever."[12] Although many pastors fear politics, through prayer politics can become a key to effective inner-city ministry. Instead of worrying that political dishonesty and "dirt" will defile us, godly men must get involved. A member of our church, Gareth Saunders, now serves on the Boston City Council. If we move according to God's Word, we will not desecrate our holy place and purpose even when working in politics.

5. *Cultural Unity.* In a world dominated by racism and discrimination, through prayer men begin to exhibit unity and peace. In following the Lord, we gain the wisdom to pray for a multiracial, multicultural manifestation of God's kingdom on earth. This requires genuine forgiveness and reconciliation grace, recognizing that our divisions hinder the world from seeing Christ. To accomplish this, we need a cultural empowerment of inner-city people. We need to lift them up without discriminating against other cultures. A multicultural expression of God's life needs to be seen and experienced in the city.

Men of Mission

"And I will be the glory in her midst."[13] Men of mission have three distinct characteristics:

1. They know the glory of God within them.
2. They reflect the glory of Christ by mirroring his character.
3. They work to the glory of God through a ministry lifestyle that attracts more men.

Men Who Know the Glory

Paul wrote, "For God, who said, 'Light shall shine out of darkness,' is the One who has shone in our hearts."[14] God's light shining in our hearts is the indwelling Christ, the hope of glory.[15] Believers under the old covenant could not touch this New Testament reality of knowing.

Men Who Reflect the Glory

Paul taught that we reflect God's glory as the Holy Spirit transforms us into the likeness of Christ.[16] Simply stated, that means we become more like Jesus. His character is summed up by the fruit of the Spirit: love, joy, peace, patience, kindness, goodness, faithfulness, gentleness, and self-control.[17] The same character must be seen through our attitudes, words, and deeds. Paul said the glory within us would be revealed one day; but the world needs to see some of it *now*.[18]

Men Who Work to God's Glory

The strength of God's inner glory leads to the pursuit of God's mission. Men work to God's glory through a ministry lifestyle in which we see ourselves as salt and light to the world. I encourage men to work as hard as they can and praise God for the results, to win others by telling about their life in Christ, and to get involved in other men's lives.

Gradually, I came to see the vision of a church without walls as the intersection of vast numbers of inner-city people empowered with spiritual, economic, social, political, and cultural strengths. They are protected by God's spirit of peace and follow his leading as they fulfill His glorious purposes.

This understanding is built on the belief that real men will respond to responsibility. As we consciously place men in positions of leadership, men of average commitment and involvement take giant strides spiritually. The end result is a river of the knowledge and experience of God's glory covering the inner city as the water covers the seas. This is the Lord's doing, and it is marvelous in our eyes.

EPILOGUE

The men who wrote the inspiring and challenging truths on this book's pages are friends of mine. Not all told of their backgrounds. Reverend Dwight Pate, for example, was addicted and homeless, living on the streets, when God saved him. Dr. A. R. Bernard sold drugs on the side to support his family while a banker, but now that Christ has come into his life he is considered one of the leading ministers in New York.

Today, unless they told you where they came from, what life was like before Christ, you would not fully realize the new creations God has made of them. That is God's work. Only God by his transcendent glory can take what was meant for evil and turn it around to make it work for His glory.[1]

Each of them in his own way can attest to the power of God to change a life, make a new man—a real man, a Christlike man—and manifest his power in their lives. These are men who are God's workmanship.

What links each of these men is that each took a little book called *Maximized Manhood*, applied its biblical principles to their lives, and it forever changed them. Because they wanted to know more, they sought out the author. We met and became friends. From that starting point, we worked together, taught and counseled with one another, and our friendships have deepened.

Yet today there is something happening in their communities, where they are a leading and vital part, and I want to acknowledge it. Principles have no color, age, or sex, so the principles of this book are for all men everywhere. Yet it would be foolish to say that because the church should have no barriers of color or culture, we cannot focus on just one segment of it.

Pastor Jack Hayford recently said the civil rights movement that sparked a slow change in the laws and attitudes of the United States was actually the cause to start a revival within the black community. But while the blacks had revival, the white established church largely sat silent. Some who called themselves Christians were obviously jealous or outright opposed to what God was doing in others' lives.

I do not want to make a mistake. I want to recognize the work God is doing in men's lives, whether it is truck drivers, a particular denomination, a group of Christian educators, or those with a different skin pigmentation. It matters little to God, but it is a matter of attention for the entire body of Christ.

God is not stagnant in his work in the world. Men of every color and race receive his grace and glory when they believe on him and trust Him. Wherever they are, I want to be part of their lives.

That is why I want to acknowledge, identify with, and be associated with such men as these. Men whose lives and ministries are making a difference in the world we live in. Men who are laying aside their pasts, traditions, and preconceptions about God, and releasing God's love, mercy, and power to bring revival and transformation to others—who are re-created into men of God.

For whatever reason you have read this book, I encourage you to read it again, recognize the truth and validity of the principles taught, and apply them to your life. Truth knows no barriers but, like soap, truth isn't effective until it's applied.

Just as these men had to dig deep into their personal lives and God's holy Word to be released into what God wanted them to be, the same is true of you. "To learn, you must want to be taught," the proverb says.[2] An ignorant man is an unteachable man. Teachability is greater than availability.

Mike Singletary playing football was an awesome man of power, feared and respected, admired and copied. But his real greatness was when he learned to forgive. The power to forgive as God forgives can only come from God. What really matters in life is God's power to obey His Word.

That only comes when we make Jesus Christ Savior and Lord in our lives. Forgiveness of sin can come from God in an instant, but the change in our lives is always a constant. Such renewal and revelation can only come from a life submitted and devoted to Christ the Lord.

Because we are not perfect, none of us will ever do things perfectly. That is why we need a Savior who is perfect to present us to God the Father in His perfection.

Champions are not men who never fail, but men who never quit. These men are champions, not because they have never failed, but because they have never quit.

Losers look at what they're going through; winners look at what they're going to. These men have been through a lot, and worked through it all because of what they saw ahead. Though they may have failed along the way, they never quit. So you also may fail at times in trying to live by godly principles, but don't ever quit. God doesn't quit on you; don't you quit on God.

We live in a "Decade of Daring," and only those who know their God will do exploits.[3] The men whose words you have just finished reading have done exploits for God and in so doing have set an example for you. They have shared with you the principles and experiences that changed and shaped their lives.

Learn from them.

ENDNOTES

Chapter 1

1. Cole, Edwin Louis, *Strong Men in Tough Times* (Orlando, Fla.: Creation House, 1993), 79.
2. Suran 19:19, Qur'an.
3. Jeremiah 33:3.
4. 2 Corinthians 5:17.
5. Jeremiah 29:11–14.
6. Matthew 16:24.
7. Acts 12:5–17.
8. Revelation 7:9.

Chapter 2

1. Genesis 1:26–27.
2. Psalm 23:4.
3. Matthew 11:30.
4. Matthew 11:28–29.

Chapter 3

1. Ezekiel 22: 24-30.
2. See 1 Corinthians 13:11.
3. Psalm 27:10 KJV.
4. Jeremiah 4:23–25.
5. Jeremiah 4:26–31.
6. Jeremiah 5:1 KJV.
7. Genesis 1:26–28.
8. Matthew 19:26.
9. Genesis 1:26.
10. Psalm 139:14.
11. Ephesians 3:20.
12. Philippians 3:13–14.
13. 2 Timothy 4:7–8.
14. 2 Chronicles 16:9.

15. 1 Corinthians 4:15 AMPLIFIED.
16. Malachi 4:6.
17. 2 Kings 2.
18. 1 Corinthians 13:11.
19. Ben Kinchlow, as quoted on back cover of Ed Cole, *Maximized Manhood* (Springdale, Penn.: Whitaker House, 1982).
20. Psalm 71:18.
21. Proverbs 13:22.

Chapter 4

1. Collosians 4:1 NIV.
2. 1 Timothy 6:1 NIV.
3. Ephesians 5:22 NKJV.
4. Ephesians 5:25 NIV.
5. Ephesians 6:1 NIV.
6. 1 Corinthians 12:3 NIV.
7. Philippians 4:4.
8. Philippians 4:12–13.
9. Matthew 28:18–19.
10. Matthew 8:8 NKJV.
11. Matthew 26:53.
12. John 19:11.
13. Joshua 1:5 NIV.

Chapter 5

1. "The War Against Women," *U.S. News & World Report*, 9 March 1994, 18.
2. The U.N. Chronicle published by the Department of Information, New York. Oct.-Dec. 1980, 55. U.N. Publications Room-A 3315, New York, NY 10017.
3. Romans 5:12.
4. Genesis 3:9.
5. Genesis 3:6.
6. Ephesians 5.
7. Genesis 3:11.
8. Genesis 38:7.

9. Genesis 38:10.
10. Genesis 38:11.
11. Genesis 38:14.
12. Genesis 38:16.
13. Genesis 38:24.
14. Genesis 38:26.

Chapter 6

1. John 20:23.
2. 1 Peter 3:7 AMPLIFIED.
3. Matthew 20:25–28.
4. Ephesians 5:25.
5. Ephesians 5:22–24.
6. Cole, *Maximized Manhood*, 23.
7. Cole, Edwin Louis, *Communication, Sex and Money* (Tulsa: Honor Books, 1987), 79.
8. 1 Corinthians 13:4–8 CEV.

Chapter 7

1. Genesis 32:24–28 CEV.
2. Hebrews 13:8.
3. 2 Corinthians 12:7–10.
4. Paraphrased from 1 Samuel 3:9.
5. Romans 12:2.
6. Romans 8:37.
7. Genesis 1:26.
8. Matthew 16:16.
9. Matthew 16:17–18.

Chapter 8

1. Romans 14:4.
2. 2 Timothy 4:7.
3. Luke 22:32.
4. Romans 8:34.
5. 1 John 2:1.
6. 1 Corinthians 13:6–8.
7. John 17:9, 20 NIV.

8. John 3:17.
9. Isaiah 64:4.
10. Matthew 13:31–32.
11. Job 23:10.
12. Romans 8:28.
13. Job 23:11–12.
14. Luke 19:10.
15. Joel 3:10 NIV.
16. Romans 8:15.

Chapter 9
1. Cole, *Maximized Manhood*, 166.
2. Matthew 10:34–36.
3. Isaiah 30:20–21.
4. Matthew 22:14, emphasis added.

Chapter 10
1. Acts 6

Chapter 11
1. Zechariah 4:10.
2. Romans 10:12.
3. 3 John 2.
4. Proverbs 21:1 NIV.
5. Proverbs 11:11.
6. Isaiah 54:17.
7. 1 Corinthians 2:9.
8. 1 John 4:4 NIV.
9. Jeremiah 29:11
10. 1 John 4:4.
11. John 3:6 AMPLIFIED.
12. Luke 16:10.
13. Malachi 2:14.

Chapter 12
1. 2 Corinthians 5:17 KJV.
2. 1 Samuel 30:1–6.

3. 1 Samuel 30:6.
4. 1 Samuel 16:13.
5. Romans 12:2.
6. Philipians 2:5.
7. 2 Peter 1:4.
8. Colossians 2:13–15.
9. Mark 11:25–26.
10. Lincoln, C.E., *The Black Church in the African American Experience* (Durham, N.C.: Duke Univ. Press, 1990), 382.
11. Ephesians 1:4.
12. Romans 13:1 NIV.
13. 1 Timothy 2:1–2.
14. Jeremiah 29:5.
15. Jeremiah 29:6.
16. Jeremiah 29:7.
17. Jeremiah 29:11.

Chapter 13

1. Hebrews 2:15.
2. 2 Timothy 1:7.
3. 2 Corinthians 5:17.
4. Romans 3:23, emphasis added.
5. Paraphrased from John 5:17.
6. Luke 15:17–18.
7. Proverbs 18:21.
8. 1 Samuel 17:46.

Chapter 14

1. Genesis 4:7.
2. Leviticus 26:8.
3. 1 Corinthians 11:1.
4. 2 Timothy 2:2.

Chapter 15

1. 2 Timothy 4:2.

2. Cole, *Maximized Manhood;* and *Communication, Sex and Money*.
3. Luke 16:1–8.

Chapter 16

1. Zechariah 2:4–5.
2. Zechariah 2:4.
3. Matthew 5:14.
4. Hebrews 12:22–23.
5. Jeremiah 29:11.
6. Habakkuk 2:14.
7. Luke 12:32.
8. John 8:32.
9. Zechariah 2:5.
10. 2 Corinthians 4:4.
11. Deuteronomy 8:18.
12. Revelation 11:15.
13. Zechariah 2:5.
14. 2 Corintians 4:6.
15. Colossians 1:27.
16. 2 Corinthians 3:18.
17. Galatians 5:22–23.
18. Romans 8:18.

Epilogue

1.Genesis 50:20.
2.Proverbs 12:1.
3.Daniel 11:32.